The Columbia River Highway
From the Sea to the Wheatfields of Eastern Oregon

by Clarence E. Mershon

First Edition: Published in 2006, including a limited edition (200) of hardcover copies.

Northwest History: Construction of the Columbia River Highway
Following in the "Footsteps of Lewis and Clark"
Oregon Cities and Towns
The Columbia River Gorge

Library of Congress Control Number: 2005933838

ISBN: 978-0-9717143-3-5 (soft cover)
ISBN: 978-0-9717143-5-9 (hard cover)

Front Cover: The photographs, starting from top left:

The Astoria Column, located in Astoria, Oregon, stands atop Coxcomb Hill. Its grafitto sculpture commemorates the discovery, exploration and settlement of the Northwest. (Photo postcard, the author.)

The Vista House, designed by Edgar Lazarus, re-opened in 2005 after a complete renovation of both its exterior and interior. The structure commands a striking view of the Columbia River Gorge. (Photo, David Sell.)

The Mitchell Point Tunnel, formerly part of the scenic Columbia River Highway, was dynamited by the Oregon State Highway Department in 1966. The destruction occurred while the Honorable Mark Hatfield served as Governor; Glenn Jackson served as Chairman of the Oregon Highway Commission.

The Umatilla County Courthouse Clock Tower is now situated on the Umatilla County courthouse grounds, Pendleton. At the urging of Dr. F.W. Vincent, the county placed the Seth-Thomas clock in a tower atop the old Umatilla County Courthouse, built in 1888, replaced in 1954.

Back Cover: **Crown Point** from Chanticleer Point, from a print by Gorge artist Charles W. Post (the author).
The Columbia River Gorge from Crown Point, from a painting by Gorge artist Charles W. Post (the author).
Shepperd's Dell, a copy of an archival photograph, courtesy of the Oregon Department of Transportation.
Multnomah Falls, the second highest waterfall in the United States (from a print, the author).

Produced and Printed in the United States of America
Guardian Peaks Enterprises
1220 N.E. 196th Avenue
Portland, OR 97230

The Columbia River Highway

From the Sea to the Wheatfields of Eastern Oregon

1913-1928

This book features photographs taken by various individuals as the magnificent Columbia River Highway was under construction (or shortly before or after). The author, former President of the Crown Point Historical Society (2000), has written six books about the communities and people of the Columbia River Gorge. Both his paternal and maternal grandfathers worked on the highway with horse teams; his father worked as a laborer and an uncle worked with a team. Because of his work in documenting the history the the area, the author has been the recipient of many photographs found in family collections of early settlers in the area. He is privileged to present many of these priceless photographs in this book.

Clarence E. Mershon

Foreword

Samuel C. Lancaster's magnificent Columbia River Highway opened the Columbia River Gorge to anyone with an automobile. From the estuary through the section affected by tides, past the Cascades, the Narrows, Celilo Falls, across the mouths of the Deschutes and John Day Rivers by bridge and traversing the dry hills beyond, the traveler could see the river much as it was described by Lewis and Clark in the expedition's journals. New towns inhabited principally by whites replaced the Indian villages experienced by Lewis and Clark, but in 1922, when the highway neared completion, the river remained much as it was a hundred fifteen years before. Lancaster wrote, "The Columbia River is peerless. Its grandeur speaks to men, and tells of Him who gathered the waters together into one place, and lifted up the mountains...I am thankful to God for his goodness in permitting me to have a part in building this broad thoroughfare as a frame to the beautiful picture which he created." The Lewis and Clark expedition descended and ascended the Columbia to establish a pathway for commerce; Lancaster provided a "Poem in Stone" along the river that opened it to all - for commerce and for pleasure.

President Thomas Jefferson's instructions to Meriwether Lewis were: "The object of your mission is to explore the Missouri River, and such principal stream of it, as by its course and communication with the waters of the Pacific Ocean, may offer the most direct and practicable water communication across this continent, for the purposes of commerce." In 1803, Captain Lewis ordered supplies and trade goods from the U.S. Government arsenal and armory at Harper's Ferry, Virginia (now West Virginia). Among the items were 40 fish gigs, 60 pipe tomahawks (some for gifts), 24 large knives, 15 rifles and associated accessories, including gun repair kits (fortunately), a small grindstone and an iron frame for a collapsible boat.

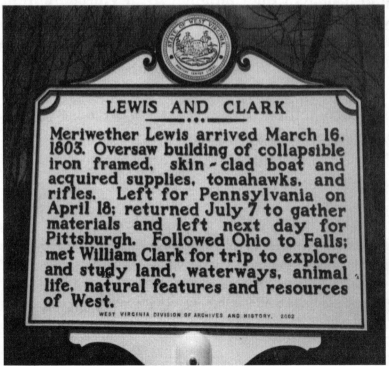

Historic Marker at Harper's Ferry, West Virginia

Replicas, Dug-Out Canoes

Replicas of dug-out canoes similar to those used by the Lewis and Clark Expedition. The canoes (at Fort Clatsop) are hewn from logs. *Photo, the author.*

The Lewis and Clark Expedition set out in May, 1804, and by late October had arrived at a Mandan village situated along the Missouri River. Nearby, on the north bank of the Missouri, Corps members built a fort in which they spent the winter of 1804-1805. The expedition resumed its journey up the Missouri in April, 1805. After portaging around the Great Falls of the Missouri, the Corps reached the three forks of the river on July 27, 1805. Proceeding up the northern-most fork, the Jefferson River, the party encountered natives of Sacajawea's tribe, which caused her "...to dance and show every mark of the most extravagant joy..." The explorers then completed their ardous trek across the Rockies and descended to the Columbia River via the Clearwater and Lewis [Snake] Rivers. The expedition reached the Columbia on October 16, 1805. The expedition encountered numerous friendly Indians who lived in settlements along the rivers. According to Captain Lewis, the presence of Sacajawea "reconsiled all the Indians as to our friendly intentions...a woman with a party of men is a token of peace." He also remarked of the abundance of salmon: "...the multitudes of this fish are almost inconceivable...the water is so clear that they can readily be seen at the depth of fifteen or twenty feet..." On October 19, commencing their voyage down the Columbia, the expedition passed the mouth of the Umatilla River (where the Columbia River Highway [later] departed from the explorers path). In descending the Columbia, the expedition encountered several rapids, some of which required a portage. Often the party's non-swimmers walked around rapids as others pushed through with the canoes. On October 21, the explorers passed the mouth of the John Day River; on October 22nd, they passed the mouth of the Deschutes and arrived at Celilo Falls. There, using ropes of elk hides, the Corps successfully lowered their canoes over the falls and by 3:00 p.m. that day, were safe below the falls with all of their canoes and baggage intact.

Captain Lewis exchanged a small canoe plus a hatchet and a few trinkets for a large "coastal" canoe. He also shot a sea otter below the falls, indisputable evidence that the ocean was near. On the 24th of October, to the astonishment of the natives, the party passed through the Narrows (called les dalles, by French voyageurs) in their canoes, again taking the precaution of having non-swimmers walk and transporting the most precious articles (papers, guns and ammunition) by land. At the Narrows, Indians lived in "large and comodious wooden houses, the

Replica, Fort Clatsop

Replica of Fort Clatsop, re-built on the site where the expedition spent the winter of 1805-1806 [burned, October, 2005].   *Photo postcard, the author.*

first such seen...since we left those in the vicinity of the Illinois..." The expedition camped below the Narrows for a couple of days to make observations, repair their canoes and hunt. In response to reports of "hostile intentions" by Indians below, expedition members readied their stock of arms and ammunition.

On October 30, 1805, the expedition came upon the "shute," or the Cascade Rapids, which presented a serious obstacle. Captain Clark and Peter Cruzatte (the party's "waterman") walked the shoreline to examine the rapids and determine the best means of traversing this stretch of the Columbia River. The "shute" and "narrow channel much compressd and interspersed with large rocks..." required a difficult portage of the canoes and baggage. The expedition took the canoes through the lower Cascades after taking the precaution of sending non-swimmers loaded with baggage by land. Below the final rapid, the explorers reached tidewater, passed Beacon Rock and progressed about 29 miles down the river, leaving the Columbia River Gorge. On November 3rd, a detachment explored the "Quicksand [Sandy] River" before continuing down river. The expedition passed "Wappato [Sauvie] Island" on November 4. Mt. St. Helens came into view, and Clark speculated (incorrectly) that is was "perhaps the highest pinical in America..."

On November 7, 1805, the expedition reached Pillar Rock. William Clark wrote in his journal, "Ocian in view! O! The Joy!" The "joy" was short-lived as near constant storms kept the Corps members from using their canoes. On November 15, the Corps camped on the north shore (Station Camp) from which both Captain Lewis and Captain Clark hiked to a point overlooking the Pacific Ocean (Cape Disappointment). Unable to find a sufficiency of game on the north shore and receiving assurances from the Chinook Indians that elk were abundant across the river, the explorers took a circuitous, upriver route to reach the south shore. On a large tree, Clark wrote, "By land from the U. States in 1804 & 1805." By New Years Day, 1806, the explorers had built cabins surrounded by a rectangular stockade, which they named Fort Clatsop, after the Indian tribe upon whose land it was built. In January, 1806, expedition members set up a salt cairn at Seaside, using five large, copper kettles in which to boil sea water to secure salt for the return trip. The expedition obtained approximately 4 bushels of salt by this method.

After spending a difficult, wet winter at Fort Clatsop and failing to make the hoped for contact with an American vessel, the Lewis and Clark expedition started its return trip up the Columbia River on March 23, 1806. Clearly Lewis and Clark had accomplished the mission set forth by President Jefferson. The explorers returned with accurate information concerning the breadth of the continent and gave impetus to what came to be called the "destiny" of the United States to occupy the land, coast to coast.

Following in the explorers "footsteps," we retrace their downriver trek in reverse and note the landmarks that they described in their journals. In 1921, when the Columbia River Highway from Astoria to Pendleton became a reality, the geological features Lewis and Clark had described could be seen. Changes, however, were apparent. Navigation locks permitted river traffic to bypass the Cascade Rapids, the Narrows and Celilo Falls. The Oregon - Washington Railroad and Navigation Company line (from Portland east) and the Spokane, Portland and Seattle tracks (from Portland to Astoria) paralleled the river. Most obvious, towns such as Astoria, Clatskanie, Rainier, St. Helens, Scappoose, Portland, Troutdale, Cascade Locks, Hood River and The Dalles replaced the native villages that had lined the river. However, within the next 50 years even greater changes occurred; the more notable features (the Cascade Rapids, Celilo Falls) disappeared beneath the impoundments of dams. However, much remains and tourists can well imagine the difficulties encountered and the remarkable achievements of the expedition as they drive between Astoria and Umatilla, following remnants of the old highway wherever possible. When driving these remnants, know that the roadbed was formed by men working primarily with hand tools, Fresnos (a type of earth mover or scraper), graders and wagons (the latter three pulled by teams of horses).

The Federal Highway Act of 1921 led to the linking of roads across state lines. A proposal regarding standards recommended by the United States Joint Board to Congress was approved in 1926. According to a Oregon Highway Commission report (8th biennial), Oregon adopted the standards in 1927-28. The Act provided for standard signs for warnings and caution, stops, distance and direction, rivers and creeks, mountain summits and elevations, historic locations and related matters. The recommendations included a numbering system for transcontinental and interstate highways that designated these routes by number. The general plan for numbering was to use even numbers beginning at the Canadian border for east-west routes and odd numbers beginning on the Atlantic seaboard for north-south routes. As a result of the Highway Commission's adoption of these standards, the Columbia River Highway (and its continuation beyond Pendleton as the Oregon Trail Highway) became U.S. Highway 30. The routes were marked by the now familiar black and white United States shield signs indicating the name of the state and the number of the route (the shields now omit the name of the state).

According to that same report (8th biennial), all sections of the Columbia River Highway had been surfaced with bituminous pavement or oiled macadam by 1928. The Warren Company formulated the paving material (Warrenite) used initially in Multnomah County to pave that section of the Columbia River Highway. This material, heated in "batch plants," hauled to the site, spread, then packed with a steamroller, is referred to as a bituminous pavement mixture. Originally, macadam referred to layers of packed gravel. Later, in order to reduce dust, hot "oil" was sprayed on the macadam as a binder, then covered with a thin layer of gravel (later, "chip seal"). On the latter, road traffic forces the gravel into the binder to create the paved surface. This type paved surface retained the name, macadam (sometimes tarred macadam or tarmac).

We may reflect upon two remarkable achievements: the Lewis and Clark expedition's exploration of the west and Samuel C. Lancaster's genius that gave the world an extraordinary marvel of engineering, the Columbia River Highway.

Dedication

The following individuals made this book possible.

Steve Lehl

For years Steve Lehl worked on a garbage route. His collecting started with historic items that he found in the refuse that his customers had discarded. He became an avid collector, particularly of photographs related to the history of the Gorge. He now works for the City of Wood Village.

Sharon Nesbit

Sharon Nesbit, writer for the Gresham Outlook, took her valuable time to review this work. Her expertise in style and custom helped the author immeasurably. Sharon, a renowned author and historian, is writing a history of Troutdale for its centennial in 2007.

George Perry VI

George Perry's father managed the Menucha estate for Governor Julius Meier. George became fascinated with history at an early age, encouraged by his mother, Joy (Crockett) Perry, a history teacher at Columbian High School, Corbett. George taught mathematics at Gresham High School until his retirement.

Charles W. Post

Charles W. Post, etcher, painter and photographer, established a portable studio (above) at Chanticleer Point in 1912. He worked there until his death in 1922. Post's photographs, paintings and sketches of scenes in the Columbia River Gorge capture the era during which the Columbia River Highway was built.

Susi Rolf-Tooley

Susi Rolf-Tooley is a consecrated Sister of the Society of St. Antony of Egypt, an Episcopal order. Her friend, the late Evelyn Cosgrove, collected the photographs included herein from her customers at the Goble tavern. After Evelyn's death, Bob Cosgrove gave the collection into Susi's keeping. Dylan Rolf digitized the photographs for the author's use.

Peg Willis

Peg Willis, Pendleton, describes herself as a "fiddler." She has an intense interest in the Oregon Trail, which crossed the Umatilla River near her home. Her interest in history is such that she drives from Pendleton to volunteer for the Friends of the Vista House at Crown Point. Her suggestions led to many improvements in this work.

The Columbia River Highway
From the Sea to the Wheat Fields of Eastern Oregon

Contents

The Columbia River Highway

From the Sea to the Wheat Fields of Eastern Oregon

The Columbia River cut a path through the Cascade Mountains, which form a nearly unbroken barrier from British Columbia to Mexico. (The Fraser River in British Columbia and the Klamath River in Northern California also cut through the range.) Early settlers and military commanders dreamt of a road that would cross Oregon from east to west. In the early 1900s, Sam Hill, wealthy attorney and entrepreneur, envisioned a road from his Maryhill estate on the north bank of the Columbia River west to Vancouver, Washington. Hill, a leader in the "good roads" movement and advocate for improved highways, served as a delegate to the first International Road Congress, held in Paris in 1908. Hill invited three other highway enthusiasts to accompany him to France: Reginald H. Thomson, Commissioner of Parks, Seattle; Major Henry W. Bowlby, noted West Point-trained engineer, and Samuel C. Lancaster, landscape engineer with prior experience in road building in the state of Tennessee. Later, both Bowlby and Lancaster would serve as staff members of the newly established highway engineering department at the University of Washington.

In Europe the group toured several countries, examining roads, aqueducts and other man-made structures on the continent. Along the Rhine River, between Koblenz and Weisbaden, they viewed terraces formed by stone retaining walls built on the steep slopes of the Rhine River gorge near Rudesheim Burg. These retaining walls, built during the reign of Charlemagne (742-814 A.D.) supported vineyards. In Switzerland, the Americans passed through the Axenstrasse, a tunnel carved through solid rock, which featured three windows from which they could view Lake Lucerne and the surrounding Alps. In Italy, the Americans found Italian stonemasons still practicing the stone-laying skills of their predecessors, the artisans who had built the retaining walls and other stonework the group had observed earlier in their travels. Hill, Thomson, Bowlby and Lancaster returned to the United States enthused and impressed by the work they had seen. They were determined to push for better roads to accomodate the increasing number of automobiles that were using roads built for wagons. Having settled in the Northwest, their efforts became centered on improving roads in Oregon and Washington.

Within the Columbia River Gorge, an ancient native-American trail connected two important trading sites, Celilo Falls and the falls on the Willamette River (which locale became Oregon City). Pioneers used this ancient (and rugged) trail to drive their livestock from The Dalles to the Willamette Valley in early days. In 1855, Lieutenant Henry L. Abbott of the U.S. Corps of Engineers wrote in his recorded observations of two "pack trails" that followed the south shore of the Columbia River. In 1868, when a telegraph line was strung connecting Portland with points east, the telegraph company followed this ancient pathway, which then became known as the "Wire Trail."

In 1856, the Oregon Territorial Legislature passed a measure that provided for a territorial road to be built from the Sandy River to The Dalles. Initially, this resulted in a wagon road between the lower Cascades (Bonneville) and the upper Cascades (Cascade Locks). In 1872, the Oregon Legislature appropriated $50,000 for the project. In 1876, the legislature appropriated another $50,000 to complete the job. Thus a very primitive road came into existence, but it was crooked, rugged and steep. During the spring freshet, the wagon road became impassable at several points. On its more western portions, spring and fall rains brought mud that hampered

Terraces Along the Rhine River

This print of the ancient ruins of Ehrenfels, shows terraces along the Rhine River in Germany built by stonemasons during the reign of Charlemagne. These retaining walls have withstood the elements for more than 1000 years. The Italian stonemasons engaged in the construction of the Columbia River Highway used similar techniques to build retaining walls to support the highway.

travel. When the Oregon Railroad and Navigation Company pushed its rail line through the Gorge in 1882-83, portions of the wagon (or county) road were obliterated.

A couple of attempts to complete a more useable road through the Gorge were initiated in 1910 and 1912, respectively. In 1910, Multnomah County started the construction of a road from Bridal Veil to the Hood River County line. A dispute with the Oregon Railroad and Navigation Company involving right-of-way stopped the effort. In 1912, the State of Oregon, Oswald West, Governor, provided prison laborers to Hood River County to construct a road around the base of Shellrock Mountain, a major obstacle to Gorge travel for decades. Because of its steep, talus slopes, rock walls meant to support the road failed and this effort, too, came to naught. A wealthy lumberman, Simon Benson, donated $10,000 for this attempt.

Benson, who made millions in the timber business with his innovations using donkey engines, railroad lines and ocean-going rafts to transport logs, became a driving force in the movement to build a road through the Gorge. Benson was among the many business and political leaders of the day who foresaw great potential for Oregon in completing a highway from Portland east. These influential men helped promote the road and often used their personal fortunes, both to overcome obstacles and to fund the construction of several ancillary projects deemed desirable, once construction was underway.

After Sam Hill failed to generate much interest in Olympia, Washington's capital, for his proposed highway through the Columbia River Gorge, he turned to business and political leaders in Oregon, where he found a much more receptive audience. Hill's interest in improving roads had led him to construct quite an extensive road system on his Washington estate. He spent more than $100,000 experimenting with various road building techniques and paving materials. Hill brought a cadre of immigrant, Italian stonemasons to Maryhill for this project. He also called upon Samuel Lancaster, who had accompanied him to Europe, to help with these experiments. In 1913, to help stir interest in the proposed highway project, Hill invited potential backers (including, in February, the entire Oregon Legislature) to his Maryhill estate to view his system of paved roads. As a result of Hill's efforts, the Legislature established the Oregon State Highway Commission and created the position of State Highway Engineer. In addition, legislation passed that authorized counties to raise money for road construction by issuing bonds. Governor Oswald West appointed lumberman Simon Benson as first chairman of the new commission. Benson and the commission promptly named Henry W. Bowlby as the commission's first highway engineer.

Meanwhile, political and business leaders were pushing for a road along the south shore of the Columbia River from Eastern Oregon to the coast. At a series of meetings, sponsored by "road improvement clubs" that had been organized in several counties, support for building the highway grew. In Multnomah County, businessman John B. Yeon garnered support for the project by addressing such clubs. This activity led to a meeting held by Multnomah County Commissioners on August 27, 1913, at the Chanticleer Inn in the Gorge. Sam Hill and other advocates of the highway spoke in support of building the highway; commissioners voted that evening to proceed with its construction. Commissioner William Lightner protested strenuously, based upon the County Surveyor's assertion that a road could not be constructed from the Summit to Latourell. An advisory board recommended that a road expert and engineer be appointed to supervise construction. On August 28, 1913, Multnomah County selected Samuel C. Lancaster as consulting engineer for the project. In September, the county turned over all engineering connected with the proposed highway to the State and set aside $75,000 for this purpose.

Lancaster immediately embarked upon a survey to determine a route for the highway through the Gorge. Impressed by the beauty he found, he later remarked:

"My love for the beautiful is inherited from my mother. When I made a preliminary survey [in the Gorge] and found myself standing waist-deep in ferns, I remembered my mother's long ago warning, 'Oh Samuel, do be careful of my Boston Fern.' And I then pledged myself that none of the wild beauty should be marred where it could be prevented. The highway was so built that not one tree was felled, not one fern crushed unnecessarily."

This same spirit inspired Lancaster to utilize the Italian stomemasons that Sam Hill had brought to his Maryhill Estate. These artisans were employed in building the stone retaining walls, arched guard rails, water stops, culverts, observation platforms and other stone structures that became such an integral part of the great highway. Lancaster explained: "Dry masonry walls [constructed without the use of cement, or mortar of any kind] have been used extensively in Germany, Italy, Switzerland and Greece in bygone centuries. We adopted this plan and constructed many miles of dry masonry walls on the steep slopes of the mountains in the Columbia Gorge. They add greatly to the charm of the highway." (Note: These artisans constructed approximately two and one-half miles of dry masonry walls with an average height of 11.5 feet.)

The result, a monument to the engineering genius of Samuel Lancaster, the vision of Sam Hill and the pragmatism, generosity and foresight of political and business leaders of the day, became world famous even before its dedication. Frederick Villiers, correspondent for the *Illustrated London News*, wrote: "It possesses the best of the great highways of the world...It is the King of Roads." Harriet Elizabeth Salt, in her book, *Mighty Engineering Feats*, ranks the highway among such other engineering marvels as the first continental railroad, the New York City water supply system, the Panama Canal, Boulder Dam, the Alaska Railroad, the George Washington Bridge and the Golden Gate and Bay bridges. Detractors, such as Commissioner William Lightner and his ally, the newly elected County Commissioner Philo Holbrook, managed, by 1915, to sever any connection Lancaster had with Multnomah County. However, by 1915, the Multnomah County portion of the highway was essentially complete. Lancaster's influence continued as the Oregon Highway Commission continued to rely upon his expertise for its planned expansion of Oregon's highway system.

In an election held on April 14, 1915, Multnomah County voters approved a bond issue of $1,250,000 to pave the highway from Portland to the Hood River County line. Lancaster chose the Warren Company's patented bitulithic paving material, Warrenite, composed of crushed rock and asphalt, to pave the road. Lancaster described the material as resilient and durable, "ideal for highways" and "the most economical and satisfactory material that can be used." Paving commenced in June and by late October, 1915, the Warren Company had completed the paving of the highway beyond Multnomah Falls. The company completed the job in the

Highway Tour

In June, 1914, Amos Benson (right) escorted a group of nineteen Columbia County leaders (including Judge Dean Blanchard, left) on a tour of the Columbia River Highway, under construction in Multnomah County.
Photo, Oregon Department of Transportation.

summer of 1916. The beautiful Columbia River Gorge was now open to a growing number of motorists. Word of the splendid highway spread quickly and motorists flocked to see the scenic Columbia River Gorge made accessible to automobile travel. The engineering genius of Samuel C. Lancaster became obvious to all who traveled the marvelous highway through the Gorge.

Public support for extension of the highway both east and west grew. Julius Meier, President of the newly formed Columbia River Highway Association, led that organization's effort to promote a Columbia River road from Astoria to Pendleton. The newly organized Oregon Highway Commission, chaired by Simon Benson, decided that the project was both feasible and needed. C.C. Chapman, publisher of the *Oregon Voter*, furthered the "good roads" movement by proposing a gasoline and automobile tax to be used for public roads. He founded the Oregon Road and Development Association, which sponsored a number of bond elections for road construction and improvements (including the Interstate Bridge [Portland to Vancouver] project). Thus, plans for a highway that would extend from Astoria to Pendleton, a distance of 340 miles, advanced with the State of Oregon involved.

On June 14, 1914, Amos Benson took a large group of road enthusiasts from Columbia County on an inspection tour of the new highway through the Gorge. The group included Dean Blanchard, Metzger, retired Columbia County Judge, John Farr, Warren, Columbia County Commissioner, Robert Yount, Rainier, President, Columbia County Good Roads Association, C.A. Nutt, Rainier, Secretary of the Association, J.G. Watts, Scappoose, L.R. Rutherford and U.S. Despain, St. Helens and C.C. Kelley, Rainier, [State] District Engineer for Columbia County. Others in the party included N.N. Blemensaadt, Andrew Clark, F.R. Davis and H.R. Dibblee representing Rainier as well as Orrin Backus, O.B. Bennett, C.L. Conyers, W.A. Hall, R.B. Magruder and Norman Merrill, representing the town of Clatskanie. This tour generated such interest in extending the highway westward from Portland that Clatsop and Columbia Counties soon issued bonds to start construction of the highway, which commenced in 1915. Hood River County also sold a $75,000 bond issue (subscribed in its entirety by Simon Benson) to finance construction of the highway eastward from the Multnomah County line. In 1915, workers completed the Mitchell Point Tunnel of many vistas, designed and engineered by John A. Elliott. Patterned after the famed Axenstrasse in Switzerland, its five "windows" provided views of the Columbia River and the Washington foothills of the Cascade Range. Thereafter, construction proceeded both east and west, though progress was impeded somewhat by a shortage of men and material during World War I.

By 1920, Oregon had 40 highway projects underway, encompassing a projected total distance of 4,458 miles. The Columbia River Highway, at 340 miles, was the furthest along; the Coast Highway, at 430 miles, was the longest. However, by that year only about 200 miles of the future Coast Highway had been graded of which about 100 miles had been graveled and about 25 miles paved. In 1920, Oregon ranked fourth among the states in money available for road purposes, behind only New York, Pennnsylvania and Illinois. Oregon leaders obviously gave the State's road program a high priority relative to other states, considering its population. In 1920, the *Fourth Biennial Report of the State Highway Commission* declared that "the improvement of the Columbia River Highway from Astoria to Pendleton is rapidly nearing completion." By 1922, the 340 mile highway would be completely graded and surfaced, with 204 miles paved and 136 miles graveled. On June 27, 1922, Simon Benson ceremoniously spread the last bit of paving material that completed the paving of the highway from Astoria to The Dalles. The ceremony, held at Rowena, near The Dalles, honored Simon Benson, not only for his role in bringing the highway into existence, but for his gifts of land for public use that continue to benefit travelers to the unique and beautiful Columbia River Gorge. Samuel Lancaster noted: "The Columbia River Highway parallels the great Continental River which Lewis and Clark explored in 1805-6, from ...eastern Oregon through the Cascade Mountains and the Coast Range to Astoria and Seaside."

The State of Oregon initiated construction of a new river-level highway east through the Gorge before World War II, but the war delayed the work. After the war, construction resumed on the project. In 1949, Governor Douglas McKay dedicated the first section of the new highway, **with assurances that the old highway would be maintained as a parkway, "perpetuating the scenic beauties for which it is justly renowned."** Despite the Governor's promise, by 1953 many sections of the highway between Dodson and Mosier had been abandoned or needlessly destroyed by highway construction. Highway tunnels at Oneonta, Mosier and Mitchell Point were filled with rubble (for the fate of the latter, see p. 179). In some places, the original stone guard rails were replaced with steel railings. In 1983, thirty-four years after Governor McKay's promise, Oregon's political leaders belatedly acted to restore and preserve some sections of the highway. In 1984, the American Society of Civil Engineers recognized the highway as a National Historic Engineering Landmark.

Seaside "Turn-Around"

The Seaside "turn-around" marked the "End of the Trail," a reference to the Lewis and Clark Expedition. The Expedition obtained salt for the return trip by boiling sea water nearby.

Photo courtesy of George Perry VI.

Seaside: Originally considered the western terminus of the Columbia River Highway, the "turn-around" at Seaside lost that status when the State Highway Commission proposed a 430-mile highway from Astoria to the California state line. Seaside, given "End-of-the-Trail" recognition by historians because of the salt cairn established there by the Lewis and Clark Expedition, was a logical choice as the western terminus of the great highway that followed in the "footsteps of Lewis and Clark" from Umatilla to the Oregon Coast.

5

Bascule Bridge Lift Span Over Young's Bay

The 227-foot Bascule Bridge, designed to span the channel in Young's Bay, under construction near Astoria, 1920.   Oregon Highway Commission photo courtesy of Dennis Wiancko.

The Highway over Young's Bay

The completed bridge and highway over Young's Bay. Highway 101 has since been re-routed, and crosses Young's Bay at a different location.   *Photo courtesy of Steve Lehl.*

Clatsop County

The Highway: Soon after its founding, the Oregon Highway Commission decided to extend the Columbia River Highway (CRH) westward to Seaside. On November 4, 1913, Clatsop County voters approved a bond issue for $400,000 for highway construction. By April, 1914, forty-six miles of roadway, much of it through standing timber, had been surveyed. As planned, Seaside became the western terminus of the CRH. From Seaside the highway paralleled the ocean beaches for twelve miles, then cut across lowlands another twelve miles into Astoria. The Warren Company paved two miles of this section (between Seaside and Gearhart) in 1914. The twenty-eight mile section from Astoria to the Columbia County line was graded in 1914. By 1915, Astoria had a "fair road" to Portland. Though paving the road started in 1917, war time (WW I) shortages of men and material as well as unusually heavy rains in 1917 and 1918 delayed completion of the project. However, work resumed in 1919 and, by 1920, the State had completed the paving of the highway from Astoria to Clatskanie. The highway in Clatsop County required a major bridge to cross the John Day River approximately 6 miles out of Astoria. At milepost 80 (from Portland) the highway reached an altitude of 700 feet at Clatsop Crest before starting its descent into Columbia County, the boundary of which was reached at milepost 74. This Astoria-to-county line segment required nine other bridges to cross creeks as well as an overpass to accomodate a railroad. The Commission also issued a contract for the construction of a 1,765-foot bridge over Youngs Bay, which was to become part of the new Coast Highway. On May 1, 1921, S.F. 'Fritz' Elfving initiated ferry service between Astoria and the Washington shore with his wood-hull ferry, *Tourist,* the first in a number of craft with that name. This service enabled residents of the Ilwaco - Long Beach area (in Washington) to reach Astoria and travel via the new Columbia River Highway to Portland. In 1925, Walter Coates initiated ferry service between Cathlamet, Washington and Westport, Oregon via Puget Island, which provided another link in the lower river transportation system. The Oregon Highway Commission purchased the Astoria-Megler ferry in 1941 and continued to operate the system until completion of the 4.1-mile Astoria-Megler Bridge in 1966.

Astoria Custom House

The Custom House in "Upper Astoria," built in 1852 to serve the burgeoning shipping industry, which developed to supply California's gold mines.

Astoria: John Jacob Astor, successful in the fur trade with his American Fur Company, organized the Pacific Fur Company in 1810. He dispatched a vessel, the *Tonquin,* to the Northwest to establish an outpost, which was to receive support from an overland expedition under Wilson Price Hunt. In 1811, the *Tonquin,* commanded by Captain Jonathan Thorn, encountered problems in attempting to cross the bar into the Columbia River, losing several crew members. However, on April 15, 1811, a landing party composed of several former Northwestern Fur Company partners, voyageurs and clerks, including

7

Duncan McDougal, David Stuart and Robert Stuart, landed on the south shore. There they established a stockade and other buildings, which they christened Fort Astoria. Captain Thorn took the Tonquin north to the vicinity of Vancouver Island where natives attacked the crew. A few crew members barricaded themselves below deck and one touched off over 4 tons of powder, which destroyed the ship and the natives swarming over its decks. However, the loss ensured that Fort Astoria would not obtain needed supplies by sea. Meanwhile, Astor's overland party made a belated appearance in January, 1812, but its members were in no condition to help supply the Fort. In 1813, because of the war with England, Astor's party sold Fort Astoria to the Northwestern Fur Company. Its directors promptly changed the fort's name to Fort George. However, the Treaty of Ghent that ended the War of 1812 required the fort to be returned to the United States. On October 6, 1818, the United States took formal possession of the area.

In 1843, J.M. Shively took up a claim in the area and platted a town. Other early settlers included James Birnie, David Ingalls, John McClure, Robert Shortess, Solomon Smith, James Welch, and A.E. Wilson. On March 9, 1847, Astoria gained a post office, reputedly the first post office west of the Rocky Mountains. The town got a boost in 1849, when it became an important trans-shipping port for goods bound from the interior to the gold mines of California. The increase in shipping led to the establishment of a customs house. Colonel John Adair,

The Astoria Column

Erected atop Coxcomb Hill in 1926, the Astoria Column (aka Astor Column) commemorates the first American settlement on the Pacific Coast. Financed by Vincent Astor, grandson of John Jacob Astor, its graffito sculpture depicts Northwest history. Photo postcard, the author.

appointed collector, couldn't secure a lot in Astoria for the facility. Consequently, he located the custom house in "Upper Astoria," which started a rivalry that lasted for several years. Also in 1849, Captains Jackson Hustler and Cornelius White started a pilot service for the Columbia River bar with the *Mary Taylor*. In 1852, James Welch and others built a sawmill in Astoria, which became the Parker Mill after its purchase by W.W. Parker. The Territorial Legislature granted the city of Astoria a charter in 1856.

In 1866, the Hume brothers, partners in the firm, Hapgood, Hume and Company, of Sacramento, California, established the first salmon cannery on the Washington shore of the Columbia River at Eagle Cliff. While sources differ, apparently Badollet and Company built the first Astoria salmon cannery in 1873. Others quickly followed, including the A. Booth & Company establishment, the Devlin and Nygant concern, the R.D. Hume facility and Kinney's firm, all built within a period of three years. By 1875, Astoria had become the salmon center of the world; twenty-four vessels laden with canned salmon cleared its harbor. In 1879, fishermen established the Fishermans' Protective Union. In 1884, a banner year, Astoria's canneries produced 620,000 cases of salmon for export. A year earlier, rail freight to the east (from Portland) opened eastern markets for Columbia River salmon. By the late 1880s, the salmon runs were in decline and, by 1890, the number of canneries had been halved. The decline brought about the consolidation of many of the remaining canneries into the Columbia River Packers' Association, organized in 1898. The Company's brand, Bumble Bee, became a market staple for consumers. Eventually, Castle and Cook, a Hawaiian Company, acquired the brand. Currently, no canneries operate in Astoria, but a labeling plant applies private brand labels for a number of firms.

On July 2, 1883, a fire swept Astoria's waterfront destroying several blocks of business houses, wharves and dwellings. A large quantity of liquor carried from the town's saloons to a "place of safety" ended up instead in "disreputable hands." Disorder and looting of many stores and houses continued for several hours. Order was restored with the help of a citizens' committee, which served notice on the hooligans to leave town within 24 hours. Though the loss was great, money from the thriving fishing industry provided the means to rebuild the town quickly. A second major fire erupted on December 8, 1922. Astoria, a city built on piling with a population of more than 14,000 people, suffered the destruction of much of the downtown area. The blaze burned for ten hours, covered 28 blocks of the business district and caused approximately 15 million dollars damage. Before the rebuilding process began, concrete bulwarks were built into which sand was pumped. This provided a more substantive foundation upon which the replacement buildings, streets and sidewalks were built. Downtown Astoria is honey-combed with tunnels beneath its sidewalks. A rash of burglaries suffered by downtown business establishments with no outward signs of forced entry reminded residents of the existence of these tunnels in later years. Another event of note occurred in 1986 when demolition crews attempted to topple the flour mill and elevators on Pier 1 (p. 12) by implosion. The charges were set and a large crowd gathered to witness the event. The explosions went off as scheduled, but the elevators remained standing. It took much more dynamite and five days work before the old structure came down, a tribute to the "built-to-last" construction practices of an earlier day.

In 1873, the *Astorian*, successor to the *Marine Gazette*, started publishing. In 1876, a telegraph line provided a communications link to Portland. An 1891 legislative act extended the boundary of Astoria to include Adairsville or "Upper Astoria." In 1898, the Astoria and Columbia River Railroad Company completed a rail line to Goble, Oregon, where it connected with the Northern Pacific line east to Portland and north, by ferry, to Tacoma.

In 1907, the Crossett Western Lumber Company, a subsidiary of the Big Creek Logging Company, purchased a large tract of timber in Clatsop County. Crossett built a mill at Wauna (p. 21) and employed more than 500 men in its logging and milling operations. C.H. Watzek managed the firm. His brother, Aubrey R. Watzek, managed the Gales Creek Logging Company, headquartered at Glenwood. Logging of timber left its mark on the scene (see p. 19).

The Astoria Column, which stands atop Coxcomb Hill, commemorates the first American settlement west of the Mississippi River. Promoted by Ralph Budd, president of the Great Northern Railway, it was erected through the generosity of Vincent Astor, grandson of John Jacob Astor, the settlement's founder. The pictorial frieze on the tower is done in graffito, a type of shallow sculpture developed by the Romans. The work traces the history of the Oregon country from legendary times before Gray's discovery to the exploration of the Northwest and the era of western migration and settlement.

Lewis and Clark: After spending a difficult winter at Fort Clatsop and failing to make a hoped for connection with an American vessel, the Corps commenced its return trip on March 23, 1806. Before leaving, the explorers circulated a notice of the expeditions endeavors among the natives and posted it at Fort Clatsop. The Captain of the American brig, *Lydia*, obtained a copy that eventually reached Washington, D.C. The expedition faced an ardous task in its return trip upriver by canoe, facing the coming spring freshet.

9

Fort Astoria (replica), 100th Anniversary

Astoria built this replica of Fort Astoria for the centennial celebration of the establishment of John Jacob Astor's post at the mouth of the Columbia River, 1811-1813.

Photo postcards courtesy of Steve Lehl.

Astoria's First Postoffice

Astoria post office, established March 9, 1847, the first west of the Rocky Mountains.

Astoria, Oregon, "Union Town"

The City of Astoria, where many building were built on piling (postmark, 1909).

Photo postcards courtesy of Steve Lehl.

City Hall, Astoria ca 1912

Astoria's former City Hall is now "home" to Astoria's Heritage Museum.

Photo postcards courtesy of Steve Lehl.

Astoria Regatta, 1912

Astoria Regatta, 12-foot speedboat class, 1912. Background, the City of Astoria.
Photo courtesy of Steve Lehl.

Astoria Docks, World War I

Astoria's Pier 1, showing grain elevators and the Astoria Flouring Mill (taken from Pier 2),
World War I era. Pier 1 and Pier 2 were completed in 1915; Pier 3 in 1921. All were built over
the opposition of Portland shipping interests. *Photo courtesy of George Perry VI.*

Astoria - Grain Storage

Stored sacked wheat for milling, Pier 1, Astoria, ca 1920.   *Photo postcard, Steve Lehl.*

Seining For Salmon In The Columbia

Seining for salmon in the Columbia River near Astoria, 1920.   *Photo postcard, George Perry VI.*

Salmon Cannery, Astoria

Cannery workers preparing salmon for canning, Astoria, 1920. In 1980, a cannery started by Samuel Elsmore, one of the more prosperous entrepeneurs in the industry, closed, ending the salmon canning business in Astoria. *Photo courtesy of George Perry VI.*

Columbia River Packer's Association Cannery

Astoria cannery, member of the Columbia River Packers' Association. *Photo postcard, the author.*

Two Million, Five Hundred Thousand Cans of Prime Salmon

2,500,000 cans of prime canned chinook salmon, Astoria (post mark, Portland, Oregon, June 2, 1909).   *Photo postcard, the author's collection.*

City of Astoria

City of Astoria before the fire of 1922.   *Photo postcard courtesy of Steve Lehl.*

Gillnets, Astoria Fishermen

Mending gillnets at Astoria ca 1920. Background: The Union Fisherman's Cooperative Packing Company, the largest salmon cannery on the Pacific Coast. After a strike by fishermen in 1896, which the packers "won," Finnish gillnetters organized and financed the establishment of the cooperative, which operated from 1897 to 1950.   Photo courtesy of George Perry VI.

"Uniontown's" New Cannery Pier Hotel

Situated on a concrete pier near the shipping channel of the Columbia River, the new (2005) Cannery Pier Hotel provides river views for its guests. The hotel, with its cannery motif, is situated where the Union Fisherman's Cooperative Packing Company (photograph above) once stood.   Photo, the author.

Commercial Street, Astoria Oregon

Commercial Street, Astoria, prior to the fire of 1922.   *Photo courtesy of Steve Lehl.*

Damage, Astoria Fire, 1922

Astoria's disastrous fire of December 8, 1922, destroyed much of the downtown area of the city. This photo shows Commercial Street [above] in the foreground.   Photo courtesy of Edith Hodgins.

Commercial Street, Astoria, 1920s

Commercial Street, Astoria, after the 1922 fire (see previous page). Andrew and Steve's restaurant, which its owners rebuilt after the fire, is now (2005) located on Marine Drive. It is owned and operated by family descendants, Gus Phillapakis and his daughter, Stephanie Dunagam. After the author partook of the restaurant's famous oyster stew, Gus kindly took him to see Astoria's underground tunnel network. Photo postcard courtesy of Steve Lehl.

Downtown Astoria, 1930s

Downtown Astoria in the early 1930s.   *Photo postcard courtesy of Edith Hodgins.*

Astoria Ferry

Astoria ferry Tourist No. 3, plying the Columbia River to upriver landings and Washington ports (postmark 1950).   *Photo postcard courtesy of Steve Lehl.*

Clear-Cutting Near Hunt Creek, Clatsop County, Creates Eyesore

Desolation from logging along the new highway led to a proposal to establish "corridors of timber" along the right-of-way to protect the natural beauty (photo near Hunt Creek in Clatsop County).   *OHC photo courtesy of Dennis Wiancko.*

Clatsop Crest

Clatsop Crest on the Columbia River Highway.   *Photo courtesy of George Perry VI.*

Bradley State Park, 1925

Bradley State Park near Clatsop Crest, ca 1925. The park is now located off of Highway 30.   *Photo postcard courtesy of Steve Lehl.*

Viewpoint on the Lower Columbia River Highway

View point, lower Columbia River Highway, mid-20s.   *Photo postcards courtesy of Steve Lehl.*

Crossett Western Lumber Company Homes, Wauna

Residences, Crossett Western Lumber Company, Wauna, Oregon, ca 1919.

21

Construction, Columbia River Highway

Construction of the highway between Clatsop Crest and Wauna.

Whitby (aka Bugby) Loops

Whitby (aka Bugby) Loops (20 miles East of Astoria), paved, 1920.

Photo postcards courtesy of Steve Lehl.

22

Columbia County, Clatskanie - Rainier

The Highway: Columbia County voters passed a $360,000 bond issue at the urging of a group of county leaders, including Judge Dean Blanchard, who had toured the new highway in Multnomah County with Amos Benson. Columbia County initiated work on the Columbia River Highway in May, 1915, after passage of the measure. Under the leadership of Simon Benson, the Oregon Highway Commission became involved and, during the biennium, 1917-18, graded and graveled the Columbia River Highway between Westport and Clatskanie. The highway between Knappa and Clatskanie had to cross Nicolai Ridge, which caused Engineer Bugby to create the Whidby (aka Bugby) loops off Clatsop Crest in order to keep within the standards set by Samuel Lancaster regarding grade and turn radii. Construction crews encountered heavy stands of timber, which made clearing a right-of-way a difficult task. In 1920, the section from Westport to Clatskanie was paved by the Warren Company. On May 27, 1919, the Department awarded a contract to the same company to pave the Clatskanie-Rainier section of the highway, which project was completed on July 31, 1920. The highway from the county line into Clatskanie required three bridges and two rail crossings, including Benson's rail line within the city limits. Twelve additional bridges were needed between Clatskanie and Rainier, including nine over Beaver Creek because the highway followed its course. The highway section from the county line to Rainier traversed about one-half the fifty-six miles across Columbia County.

A substantive section (approximately 7 miles) of the original highway (now Beaver Falls Road) lies between Clatskanie and Rainier. Completed in 1918, the roadway is narrow, with an average 20-foot width plus 2-foot shoulders, the original configuration. It has numerous sharp curves and crosses Beaver Creek eight times in the corridor. Five of the eight original bridges are extant though nearly all of those surviving have suffered some damage. Beaver Falls Road is now owned and maintained by Columbia County, which has replaced three of the section's original bridges. Because the highway remains essentially as constructed, with visible engineering features of the original highway intact, it is worthy of preservation and restoration.

Clatskanie: Clatskanie takes its name from a band of Indians, the Klatskanis (or Tlatskanais) who lived upstream from Astoria. The tribe had migrated to the lower Columbia River from north of the river. Before the Columbia River Highway came through, Clatskanie was a bustling hamlet with three hotels, four mercantile and grocery stores, a meat shop, Mrs. Haines' Home Bakery, a music store, a photography shop, a blacksmith shop and many other commercial establishments. Hilliard's Cafe and the Grand Central and Panama Hotels served hearty meals. Elsie Markwell sold yard goods that her mother, without patterns, made into well-fitted clothing for her customers. The Blacford family provided the residents with Clatskanie's own newspaper, the *Clatskanie Chief*. A power plant on Fall Creek provided electricity. Twice each week, the paddle wheel steamer, *Beaver*, stopped at the dock to bring supplies and take on cargo. The town had both a men's and women's clothing store and, of course, seven or eight saloons. Because of its location along the lowlands bordering the Columbia River, some of the town's buildings were built on piling. In 1920, Clatskanie boasted 1,171 residents. That year, W.J. Silva, native of Rainier, retiring from active service as a steamboat captain, opened a garage in Clatskanie with his brother, J.W. Silva.

Three industries dominated the local economy: lumbering, fishing and agriculture. The (Simon) Benson Timber Company's camp close by provided jobs as did the West Oregon camp on the old Nehalem Road. Palm's Mill, to the west, and several small shingle mills also provided work. Though salmon runs had declined from earlier times, fisherman still used gill and seine nets to make a living. The extensive lowlands in the area provided farmers with a rich soil, compared by some to the diked lowlands in The Netherlands, and the Clatskanie-based Columbia Agricultural Company supported that endeavor. Simon Benson first entered the timber business in Columbia County. He sold his timber business when his wife became ill, and moved to Colville, Washington, a drier climate. In 1890, after Benson's wife, Esther, passed away, he returned to Oregon to re-enter the timber business. He entered into a partnership with Ordway and Weidler, to whom he had been selling logs. The partners purchased a large tract of timber and built a logging railroad to transport logs from the woods. When the price of logs declined, both of Benson's partners decided to leave the business and each sold his interest to Benson. Benson, always an innovator, experimented with using donkey engines to yard logs, which practice he soon perfected. Sensing an opportunity in California's development, Benson purchased a mill in San Diego to supply that burgeoning market. However, that created a problem; how to supply the mill with logs considering the exorbitant costs to ship logs either by rail or ship. Local historians credit the Company's accountant, O.J. Evenson, with the idea of transporting logs by raft.

The Benson Timber Company's railway through Clatskanie carried the firm's logs to the Wallace Slough. There the company built a huge "cradle" at dockside in which logs were laid and laced together with chains. The first "raft," pulled by an ocean-going tug, carried more than three million board feet of logs to San Diego in twenty days without mishap. Other rafts carrying logs to San Pedro, California, followed. Because of their shape, these rafts came to be called "cigar log rafts." Thus Benson's company supplied much of the lumber for Southern California's building boom at the turn of the century. The innovation saved Benson Timber Company thousands of dollars in transportation costs and made Simon Benson a very wealthy man.

Rainier: The City of Rainier is situated where a Chinookan tribe, the Katlamoiks, had a village. A second tribe, the Katlagulaks, had a village close by. In 1848, according to local historians, a mate on a sailing vessel staked a claim on the south shore of the Columbia River, which he placed with a friend, Peter Crawford, for safekeeping before sailing on. When the mate failed to return, Crawford gave the claim to his friend, Charles E. Fox. Fox "proved" the claim, which he and Crawford then surveyed and platted (1850-51). Fox named the townsite Rainier after Mount Rainier in what is now Washington State. According to Grace Reid, *Columbia County History*, Volume XII, 1973, Fox "was a man of many ideas, but did not follow through...building a grist mill before he thought of the fact that there was no grain for miles around." In 1863, a man with ideas and "follow through" settled in Rainier where he acquired a sawmill on the waterfront. Soon, Dean Blanchard owned a country store, a city dock, warehouses, a river boat and a pile driver. Blanchard was also active in politics, holding both city and county offices, including a judgeship. Rainier became an incorporated city under State law in 1885.

When the highway came through, Blanchard's sawmill had closed, though lumbering and fishing remained viable industries. The Portland-Astoria railway line provided a transportation link both to the interior and to the coast. The highway commission paved the Rainier-Deer Island section of the CRH in 1920. A small section (.9 mile) in the town itself was not paved until 1921. In 1920, Rainier's population had declined to 1,287 from 1,359 ten years earlier. For several years "Windy" Hayes had operated a ferry system that connected Rainier, Oregon and Longview, Washington, but which he discontinued in 1922. In August that year, the Long-Bell Lumber Company hastened to provide ferry service for its Oregon employees with a barge. The company soon ordered two ferries built, *Oregon* and *Washington,* from Hamlin F. McCormick's St. Helen's Shipbuilding Company, to use in ferrying workers, passengers and automobiles between Rainier and Longview. In 1920, Rainier's newspaper, the *Rainier Review*, was edited by A.E. Veatch.

Columbia River Highway, Clatskanie

The newly paved Columbia River Highway into Clatskanie provided an all-weather route for traffic to and from the coast.   *Photo postcard courtesy of Steve Lehl.*

Lowland Farm, Clatskanie

A view of the Columbia Agricultural Company's Clatskanie farm from the Columbia River Highway.   *Photo courtesy of George Perry VI.*

Clatskanie, Oregon

The City of Clatskanie, which in 1921 boasted 1,171 residents.

Main Street, Clatskanie

Main Street, Clatskanie, Oregon, 1920s.   *Photo postcards courtesy of Steve Lehl.*

Clatskanie, Oregon - Waterfront

The Clatskanie waterfront, E.L. Edgerton General Store (center).   *Photo courtesy of Steve Lehl.*

A Benson Raft Ready For Its Ocean Voyage

Simon Benson's "cigar" log raft of six million feet bound for San Pedro, California. The "cradle" used to form the rafts can be seen, background, right.   *Photo postcard, the author.*

Logging Columbia County Forests

A load of Columbia County logs destined for trans-shipment from the Columbia River.

Photo courtesy of George Perry VI.

Rainier School

Rainier Public School, Rainier, Oregon.   *Photo courtesy of Susi Rolf-Tooley.*

The Railroad Line Through Rainier

Main Street, Rainier, Oregon, 1920s.   *Photo courtesy of Susi Rolf-Tooley.*

Main Street, Rainier, Oregon, Mid-1920s

On Rainier's Main Street, the Bungalow Restaurant, the Commercial Hotel, Rader's Ice Cream shop and a harness shop are visible.   *Photo postcard, Steve Lehl.*

The Ferry, *Oregon*, Rainier to Longview, Mid-1920s

The ferry, Oregon, *transported automobiles and passengers between Rainier and Longview, Washington. A sister ferry,* Washington, *is docked to the left. Both ferries were built in St. Helens, Oregon.* Photo courtesy of Susi Rolf-Tooley.

Hammond Lumber Company Rail Line, Rainier

Hammond Lumber Company Railway, Rainier. *Photo postcard courtesy of Steve Lehl.*

Columbia County - Goble, St. Helens, Scappoose

The Highway: From its early start in 1915, construction of the CRH proceeded in subsequent years, though work slowed considerably during the war (World War I) years. By 1920, the Deer Island-Scappoose section had been completed and paved. Engineers had to take the highway across Prescott Point between Rainier and Goble. The result gave travelers an extraordinary view of the Columbia River from Prescott Point and a marvelous scenic descent into Goble past Little Jack Falls, which became a wayside stop along the way. From Goble to Scappoose and beyond to the Columbia-Multnomah County line, the highway traversed flat country that supported many farms, particularly dairies. It passed through the county seat, St. Helens, and Scappoose. The highway required ten bridges from Goble to the county line. Governor Oswald West appointed former Columbia County timber baron Simon Benson to chair the newly established Oregon Highway Commission after the legislature established the department. Benson's leadership gave Oregonians and visitors a splendid highway from Seaside to Pendleton as well as plans for a state-wide system of highways. His philanthropy gave the public a beautiful park area near Multnomah Falls and other amenities, such as the Benson footbridge at Multnomah Falls and numerous ancillary projects such as stonework along various trails that enhance the experience for those who visit the Gorge. By 1920, the CRH, from Astoria to Portland, was (essentially) paved.

Goble: According to local historians, on October 15, 1884, the first locomotive "chugged its way [from Portland] through the timber to Hunter's Landing, near Goble." A preliminary survey for the line had been completed in 1871, but the project languished for more than ten years. In 1883, however, the line across the Cascade Mountains through Stampede Pass was "rushed to completion," which connected Tacoma with the eastern terminus in Minnesota. The line to Portland, however, depended upon the completion of the ferry, *Tacoma*, which was to be used to transport trains across the Columbia River. After the ferry was launched, transcontinental trains could continue southward from Tacoma to Kalama, Washington, there to be transported by ferry to Hunter's Landing, thence on to Portland. To handle the trains, engineers designed a ferry slip that rose and fell with the river's level so that trains could be loaded and unloaded expeditiously regardless of its level.

The Oregon slip was moved to Goble, Oregon in 1890. *Tacoma* could ferry up to 21 box or passenger cars as well as a "road" and a switch engine. Regular service between Kalama and Goble continued from 1890 to 1908, when the Northern Pacific's railroad bridge across the Columbia River connected Vancouver, Washington and points north with Portland. In 1891, John A. Hurlburt completed a survey for a rail line from Goble to Astoria. The city of Astoria contracted with A.B. Hammond and E.L. Bonner to complete the extension of the railway in 1896, but the line was not completed until 1898. Though Goble had a station on this railroad, the demise of its rail link to Kalama ended the town's glory days as a principal station for the Northern Pacific. However, Martin Horan started a ferry service and Jack Reid converted a couple of fishing boats to carry passengers between Goble and Kalama so that Astoria to Puget Sound passengers could avoid the "loop" through Portland. Reid soon put a 100-passenger ferry, *Queen*, into service and, in 1923, after the highway was completed, put *Elf*, which carried automobiles and freight, into service. Ferry service terminated in 1934 after completion of the Rainier-Longview bridge ended the need for the Goble-Kalama "transfer" business. The Northern Pacific/Great Northern combine purchased the Astoria and Columbia Railroad in 1907 and, in 1911, made it part of the Portland Division, Spokane, Portland and Seattle Railway. The

Astoria and Columbia carried thousands of passengers between Portland and Astoria until the completion of the CRH in 1920, after which traffic began to to decline gradually, but signficantly.

Because of its position as a transfer point for the Northern Pacific, Goble became quite a large and busy town. Harvey M. Fowler, born in St. Helens in 1859, ran a wood yard in Prescott, Oregon, furnishing cordwood for river steamboats. In 1881, he took up a homestead of 160 acres west of Goble and a pre-emptive claim of 160 acres along the Clatskanie River. In 1893, he built a large general store in Goble that he operated until his death in 1918. In 1919, his son, C.F. Fowler, purchased the store from his mother, Flora A. (Archibald) Fowler. The store handled groceries, feed, gas, oil and other items for the local trade and served as the post office. In 1926, C.F. Fowler succeeded his mother as postmaster of Goble. Another individual who contributed much to the economy of Goble was Frank Warren. In 1895, after a way of preserving fresh salmon was found, Warren built a large cold storage plant on the river and shipped iced salmon by rail across the country. The plant closed about the time that catching salmon in fish traps was outlawed by the State of Oregon. It burned in 1931. Nearby, the Columbia River Lumber and Fuel Company established a lumber camp, built a 12-mile flume to the river, put in a mill and employed some 200 men. After the Goble, Nehalem and Pacific Company purchased the mill site, the firm salvaged a number of buildings and painted them red. As a consequence, the town became known as "Red Town." The Company built a store with a large, second-story dance hall. An excursion boat brought revelers from Portland and dances lasted all night. Some maintain that the name "Red Town" came about because of the activities of the revelers, not the red paint. Members of a local Grange petitioned to have the town's name changed officially to Beaver Homes.

St. Helens: St. Helens is built on the site of a native village of the Nayakaukaues. It was first known as Wyeth's Rock for an early trader, Nathaniel J. Wyeth, who built a post, Fort William, on a nearby site (Sauvie Island) in 1834. Earlier that year, Wyeth had established Fort Hall on the Snake River in Idaho. He hoped to gain some advantage vis a vis the Hudson Bay Company in the fur trade. Francis A. Lemont first came to the area in 1929 on the brig, *Owyhee*, which crossed the bar and ascended the Columbia River to Deer Island. The ship stayed in the area through the summer of 1830, trading with the natives and putting up salmon. During the year that the *Owyhee* remained, a devastating measles epidemic broke out, which seemed to have started amongst the Indians in the immediate proximity of the ship. The epidemic spread throughout the region, up and down the river and along the coast. Entire villages were wiped out by the disease. When Lewis and Clark descended the river some 25 years earlier, approximately 800 members of the Multnomah tribe lived on the upper end of Sauvie Island. The epidemic of 1829 caused such devastation to this village that by 1835 not a single member of the tribe survived. Natives believed that Captain John Dominis of the *Owyhee* had emptied a jar of "bad medicine" into the river that caused the outbreak. Only the intervention of Dr. John McLoughlin prevented the Indians from harming the ship's crew. While anchored in the area, the crew put up fifty casks of salted salmon, which sold in Boston for ten cents per pound upon the ship's return there, presaging future events..

In 1847, Captain Henry M. Knighton took a donation land claim in the area, platted a town site and built a wharf. He named the town, Plymouth, but changed the name to St. Helens, after the mountain in view to the northeast. In 1849, Captain Francis A. Lemont returned to St. Helens as master of the brig, *John Davis*. The ship took on a cargo to take to the booming gold rush city of San Francisco, where Lemont sold both the cargo and the ship. He then returned by ship as a passenger to settle in St. Helens. In 1850, recalling his experiences of an earlier day, he established a salmon preserving plant, purchased salmon from the natives and sent his product to market by ship. In 1852, the Pacific Mail Steamship line built a wharf and warehouse on the

Columbia River for its ships. At one time, town leaders thought that St. Helens might become the dominant port along the Columbia River. However, fires caused heavy losses in the town and discouraged many. Oliver Meeker, brother of Ezra, who had marked the Oregon Trail, owned docks on the river that burned. He rebuilt, only to lose his holdings again to fire. In 1883, the Muckle brothers owned a mill, a store and a river boat. The fire of 1904 destroyed their holdings. The Oregon Legislature gave St. Helens its charter in 1889. In 1906, Columbia County erected a courthouse that still stands on the waterfront.

In 1907, Ernest H. Meyer opened a St. Helens office for the McCormick Lumber Company, an affiliate of the McCormick Steamship Company. In 1909, Hamlin F. McCormick purchased the former Muckle Brothers mill site. In 1910, his St. Helens Lumber Company started production and by 1912 had a payroll of $100,000 per month. The city granted McCormick a 35-year franchise to provide electric power to the area. From 1900 to 1910, St. Helen's population increased from 258 to 742; in the next decade it increased to 2,220. In 1912, McCormick decided to start the St. Helens Shipbuilding Company. On October 12, 1912, his firm launched its first ship, *Multnomah*. Others followed, including *Merced, Celilo, Wampana* and *Everett*. Production continued with the motor ships, *City of Portland, S.A. Allard* and *City of St. Helens* and, during World War I, the yard built two vessels for the United States government. After the war, as steel hulls replaced wooden hulls, the yard made smaller craft until it closed when the onset of the depression dampened demand. McCormick started other business ventures, including the St. Helens Tie and Lumber Company, a creosoting plant that produced railroad ties, and the St. Helens Wood Products Company, which utilized waste from other mills to make broom handles and lath. Hamlin McCormick's holdings eventually became Pope and Talbot.

In 1881, James Muckle started a newspaper in St. Helens, which consolidated with another to form the St. Helens' *Sentinental Mist*. In 1921, S.C. Morton edited the newspaper, published as the *Columbia County Mist*. Charles Wheeler is credited with bringing rail service to the St. Helens' industrial area, which encouraged development. In 1926, William P. Hawley built his St. Helens Pulp and Paper Company plant and, in 1930, another mill, the Fir-Tex Insulating Board Company, came to the area. Another firm, the St. Helens-based Western Cooperage Company, made barrel staves that were shipped to barrel manufacturers across the country. Later, the company relocated to the community of St. Johns in North Portland.

Scappoose: The first post office, Columbia, was located in Samuel T. Gosa's store at Johnson's Landing. In 1872, the post office became Scappoose, but remained at Johnson's Landing. By 1884, a railroad line had been built from Portland as far as Hunter's Landing. In 1886, William W. West platted a new town, gave several acres of land for a railroad depot on the new rail line and built a general store. The Scappoose post office was moved to the new location, which essentially relocated the town. West's son, Jared, managed the store, which, in 1888, sold to J.G. Watts and D.W. Price. Watts and Price moved the store across the street. In 1894, when West platted more property in the business district, the partners purchased four lots and built a larger store. The new building had an upstairs hall that was used for lodge meetings and other functions. The railroad depot, post office and store became the center of the town of Scappoose.

The Columbia County bottomland along the Columbia River provided ideal grazing land for cattle, and dairies flourished. Another of West's sons, Harry, took a donation timber claim of 160 acres. He logged the property, cleared the land and started a dairy. He traveled to the Jersey Islands to acquire thoroughbred stock for his herd. He built a 56-by-84-foot dairy barn for 80 head with storage capacity for 200 tons of hay. His Jersey stock took many awards and his cattle auctions attracted buyers from throughout the country. Alex H. Bonser, born August 21, 1857, on Sauvies Island, started a herd of purebred Ayrshire cattle, operating a 260-acre farm (later, the Columbia River Highway ran through his land). Antone Barber imported stock from his native Poland and established a lowland dairy that made him a wealthy man. The Rainier creamery, established in 1888, produced Jewell Ice Cream, which became a well-known Oregon brand. In 1890, Albert Johnson purchased several hundred acres along the Multnomah Channel and established a large Holstein-Friesian herd. The Johnson family operated this dairy for nearly a century. P.A. Frakes also built up a herd of Holstein-Friesian cattle in the same area. His registered Holsteins took many awards, including significant recognition of his stock at the 1905 Lewis and Clark Exposition in Portland. His large barn became a landmark in the Scappoose area. His cattle auctions also attracted many buyers to Scappoose. In the 1890s, Gus Hegle established a dairy farm and creamery that became the Oak Grove Creamery. His products won many quality awards and his butter found a ready market in Portland restaurants and hotels.

Thomas Jackson took a donation land claim along Jackson Creek, where he lived only a few years. A relative took over the claim, which was later purchased by Thomas W. Johnson. Johnson established a dairy herd, constructed a large barn and built a water-powered creamery. Johnson and his son, Calvin, added a store at which nearby settlers could purchase needed items and sell their milk and cream. The Fairview Pioneer Cemetery is situated on land formerly part of the Johnson's holdings. Later, P.A. Frakes and his son, George, bought the Johnson creamery and integrated it into their dairy business. Wesley L. Brown purchased the dairy farm in the 1940s and operated a dairy with Holstein-Friesian stock into the 1960s. Brown's daughter, Bunnette (Brown) Looney and other descendants continue to live on parcels separated from the original acreage. The family's old farmhouse, beautifully renovated, remodeled and restored, is now (2005) owned by Larry C. Etzel. Unfortunately, the historic barn (p.50) is gone.

In 1920, Joe Fisher established the Scappoose Creek Dairy on 400 acres near the present location of the airport (formerly located on the CRH). He built the large barn for his herd of Holstein-Friesian dairy cattle. In the 1990s, subsequent owners, Glenn and Shirley Cave, restored the exterior of the barn (see p. 50), renovated the home and outbuildings and started a bed and breakfast business. Unfortunately, the couple died in an aircraft accident in Alaska. The business is now owned and operated by Duane and Renee Pizzo, who continue to improve the property. (Their restaurant, the "Josephine" is [2005] worthy of a visit!) They plan to renovate and remodel the interior of the barn and the milk house. Another old barn located on West Lane Road (formerly the CRH) was purchased by Gus Wagner in the late 1930s. Wagner used the barn to house horses and a herd of registered Aberdeen-Angus cattle, which grazed his 300 acres. At one time, the property was the site of a blockhouse built to protect settlers from possible Indian attacks (that did not occur) and a school.

In 1888, when James G. Watts and his brother-in-law moved the former West store across the street from its former location, Watts became postmaster and an agent for the Northern Pacific Railroad at its Scappoose office. Elected Columbia County Clerk in 1898, he was instrumental in paying off a large deficit and building a surplus that permitted construction of a new courthouse. In 1900, he designed and built a lovely Victorian-style home for his wife, Arizona (Ewing) Watts, and their three children. In 1920, city founders met in the Watts residence to write a city charter and residents elected James G. Watts as the first Mayor of Scappoose. Scappoose became an incorporated city in 1921. This nearly coincided with the completion of the Columbia River Highway through the town. In 1920, reflecting the times, two garages were built in Scappoose, one by Tony Barber; another by Charles Wikstrom. Soon, Scappoose's first gasoline station was built by Charles Koutek at the corner of Railroad Avenue and Casey Street. Sections of the original CRH exist (in 2005) as the old Portland Road and the West Lane Road. The former Watts residence is now the Scappoose City Hall and is also the home of the local historical society.

Prescott Point

Prescott Point overlook, Columbia River Highway.   *OHC photo courtesy of Dennis Wiancko.*

Scenic Stretch, Lower Columbia River Highway

The descent from Prescott Point to Little Jack Falls, Columbia County. This section was paved in 1920.
                                          Photo postcard courtesy of Dave Sell.

35

The CRH West of Little Jack Falls

Above: The Columbia River Highway between Prescott Point and Little Jack Falls shortly after the stretch was paved. Below: The old highway (same location) is now strewn with rocks and overrun with brambles, but does provide a difficult path to reach the falls. The cooling tower (demolished in May, 2006) for the Trojan nuclear power plant is visible in the background.

Top photos: Cross & Dimmit postcard courtesy of Dave Sell; lower photo, the author.

Little Jack Falls

The approach to the scenic wayside at Little Jack Falls on the original CRH (Left). Right, Little Jack Falls during the spring freshet.

Photo (left) courtesy of Steve Lehl; photo (right), courtesy of Susi Rolf-Tooley.

Kalama, Washington, to Goble, Oregon, Rail Ferry

The Northern Pacific Railroad's ferry, Tacoma, *Kalama to Goble.*

Photos courtesy of Susi Rolf-Tooley.

Goble, Oregon, and the Rail Lines to the Ferry Slip

On left, the Goble Hotel, Hunter's Saloon, a barber shop, Molly Hunter's restaurant and boarding house,the train depot and the Warren Packing Company cold storage plant.

Photos courtesy of Susi Rolf-Tooley.

Goble, Oregon, 1910

Above, Dick Link's store and home (2nd story), Henry Welter's meat market, H.M. Fowler's general store, the post office and Alfred Hunter's home (diapers on line)

Goble, Oregon, 1915

Above: Margaret 'Mamie' Welter drives an early Packard truck ca 1915. Below, a view of Goble looking north toward the Columbia River. Photos courtesy of Susi Rolf-Tooley.

Business District, Goble, Orgon

Above: The "Berlin," docked at the Warren Packing Company's cold storage plant, Goble, Oregon, 1924. Below: Harvey M. Fowler's general store, which he built in 1893. Fowler is 4th from the left; Lawrence Archibald stands to his left; C.F. Fowler is beyond the post (under the "F" in "office"); next right is "Mr. Blake." The others are not identified.

Photos courtesy of Susi Rolf-Tooley.

Warren Company Crusher, Goble

Warren Construction Company crusher at Goble, used in the construction of the Columbia River Highway.   *Photos courtesy of Susi Rolf-Tooley.*

Road Crew, Columbia County, 1915

Road crew working on the Columbia River Highway near Goble, 1915.

Inspecting Work on the Columbia River Highway

The Columbia County Court's Roadmaster, Leo G. Titus, appointed January 6, 1915, inspects work on the highway. The driver of the 1914 Model-T Ford is not identified.

Grading the Columbia River Highway Near Goble, 1915

CRH road crew (county employees), near Goble, Oregon, 1915.

Photos courtesy of Susi Rolf-Tooley.

The Columbia River Highway at Goble

The Columbia River Highway near Goble, mid-1930s.   *Photos courtesy of Susi Rolf-Tooley.*

The Goble Tavern on the Columbia River Highway

The Goble Tavern in the 1930s - the Columbia River Highway in the foreground. (The automobile is a 1936 or 1937 General Motors, probably a Chevrolet.)

Beaver Homes (aka Red Town)

Beaver Homes (aka Moorseville and "Red Town"), located south of Goble, Oregon).

Photos courtesy of Susi Rolf-Tooley.

Columbia River Highway, Columbia City, Oregon

The CRH through Columbia City, Columbia County, Oregon (early 1920s).

Columbia City, Oregon

Street scene at Columbia City, Oregon.   *Photo postcard courtesy of Steve Lehl.*

CRH Bridge Over Willow Creek

Concrete viaduct over Milton Creek near St. Helens, completed in 1920. Columbia River Highway.   *OHC photo courtesy of Dennis Wiancko.*

St. Helens Waterfront

Business section, St. Helens waterfront, 1912.

Main Street, St. Helens, Oregon

Main Street, St. Helens, Oregon (a few years later than the photo above, probably taken in 1916 or 1917).   *Photo postcards courtesy of Steve Lehl.*

McCormick's St. Helen's Shipyard

Hamlin F. McCormick's St. Helens shipyard, which launched several wooden ships from 1912 through the 1920s. The yard had 4 ways. *Photo postcards courtesy of Steve Lehl.*

Laying The Keel

Laying the keel for a large, ocean-going, wood-hulled ship.

47

City of St. Helens, Oregon

Residential area, St. Helens, Oregon. The Columbia County court house (center right), built in 1906, remains a landmark in St. Helens.   *Photo postcard courtesy of Steve Lehl.*

St. Helens Waterfront

St. Helens is situated on the Columbia River near the downriver end of Sauvies Island. At one time, its promoters hoped that St. Helens would become the major port on the river.

Photo postcard courtesy of Steve Lehl.

Sawmill Complex, St. Helens

Sawmill complex, St. Helens, Oregon, 1930s.   *Photo courtesy of Steve Lehl.*

Joe Fisher's Scappoose Creek Dairy

Joe Fisher owned 300 acres on which he ran a herd of Holstien-Friesian dairy cattle for which he built this barn in 1920. The current owners, Duane and Renee Pizzo, have a bed and breakfast business and also operate a restaurant located in the renovated old farm home.

Photo courtesy of Duane and Renee Pizzo.

The Restored Fisher Barn, Scappoose

A beautifully restored Scappoose barn (ca 1920) near the airport, Scappoose (see story p. 34)
.   *Photo, the author.*

Dairy Herd, Scappoose, 1920

Johnson's Columbia County (Scappoose) Dairy Herd ca 1920 (see p. 34).

Photo courtesy of George Perry VI.

Multnomah County-Portland

The Highway: Oregon business, professional and political leaders took an active part in transportation affairs, particularly in promoting and giving impetus to the Multnomah County Commission's decision to construct a highway through the Columbia River Gorge. Simon Benson and his son, Amos Benson, John F. Carroll, Rufus Holman, C.S. Jackson, Julius Meier, H.L. Pittock, Frank Terrace, Governor Oswald West and John B. Yeon joined in an effort to encourage public acceptance of the project and to provide the funds necessary to build the road. Sam Hill had experimented with various highway construction techniques on his Washington estate. Through his contacts, Hill had found an engineer, Samuel C. Lancaster, with the experience and expertise to direct the work. Lancaster had supervised the experimental highway work on Hill's estate. Hill believed that Lancaster could turn his dream of a highway through the Gorge into a reality. Upon Hill's recommendation, Multnomah County hired Lancaster as consulting engineer to locate and design the highway and to supervise its construction. Lancaster quickly named John B. Yeon as Roadmaster to oversee the actual construction and to manage the road crews engaged in the work. Lancaster described Yeon as "a wealthy and public-spirited citizen of Portland [who] volunteered to give, without remuneration, his entire time to this splendid work; and his offer was quickly accepted. Mr. Yeon's long experience in handling men in lumber camps fitted him admirably for this great task. His sagacity and love of the beautiful enabled him to grasp the meaning of the Engineer's plans, and thus to decide important matters correctly and with great dispatch." Multnomah County taxpayers paid for the Multnomah County section of the highway and continued to pay for its improvement and maintenance through 1920.

Lancaster undertook his survey immediately after being hired on August 28, 1913. Roadmaster Yeon established the first construction camp at Multnomah Falls in October. Other camps along the route soon followed. In April, 1915, Multnomah County voters approved a bond measure to pave the newly christened Columbia River Highway to the county line. The Warren Company gained the contract and paving commenced in June, 1915; by late October that year, the highway was paved beyond Multnomah Falls. People immediately took to their automobiles to see the scenic wonders of the Columbia River Gorge. These visitors recognized the measures Lancaster had taken to protect the natural beauty of the area; miles of roadway supported by stone retaining walls and viaducts that took the highway along sensitive slopes. These features and others bore witness to Samuel Lancaster's engineering genius that made a highway through Gorge possible. As mentioned earlier, Frederick Villiers quite appropriately declared the Columbia River Highway the "**The King of Roads**."

Initially, officials classified certain roads from Portland as "access roads" to the highway. However, "Field Notes" completed by F.N. Drinkhall, Oregon State Highway Department in 1924, documents the highway's path through Portland. The highway passed through Linnton into Portland along the west bank of the Willamette River quite similarly to its later configuration. However, to reach milepost 0.0, it came via N.W. Thurman and 16th Avenue to Burnside, then east via S.W. Washington to Broadway. From milepost 0.0 (at Broadway and Washington) a traveler continued three blocks eastward to 4th Avenue, took 4th north to Burnside and turned east on Burnside to cross the Willamette River. Once on the east side, the highway continued east on Burnside to 39th Avenue, then turned south to Stark Street. According to Drinkhall's notes, Stark Street (Baseline Road) was the route to reach the Columbia River Highway. Perhaps in response to the adoption of recommended standards approved by Congress in 1926, the Columbia River Highway became U.S. 30. In any case, the official route of the highway through Portland, west to east, became St.

Helens Road to Wardway, thence via N.W. Vaughn to N.W. 19th. The highway followed 19th to Burnside, thence east on Burnside to S.W. Washington Street, which took the traveler to milepost 0.0 at S.W. Broadway. From here, Highway 30 followed Washington to 4th, 4th to Burnside, thence east on Burnside. A change in the original route occurred at the intersection of Burnside with N.E. Sandy Boulevard. The highway followed Sandy Boulevard northeastward to what is now Parkrose, then continued east on the Sandy Road to reach Troutdale. From Troutdale, the highway followed the east bank of the Sandy River to reach the Stark Street Bridge (the original start of the Columbia River Highway).

In 1926, developments to improve the route(s) of the highway through Portland occurred. Multnomah County voters approved a bond measure that provided funds for several projects, including four related to the highway. One involved the widening and straightening of St. Helens Road from N.W. Portland through Linnton ($400,000). A second provided for the paving of Columbia Boulevard from St. Johns east to its junction with the Sandy Road (Sandy Boulevard - $80,000). A third project to widen Sandy Road from the city limits to the Fairview-Gresham Road (Fairview Avenue, now 223rd Avenue) received $200,000. Finally, the measure provided $12,000 to pave Section Line Road (Stark Street) from 82nd Avenue to Fairview Avenue. These projects improved the two major routes that took the highway into Portland from the east (Sandy Road and Stark Street) as well as St. Helens Road, the route from Portland to the "lower" Columbia River Highway. Additionally, paving Columbia Boulevard from the Sandy Road to St. Johns would later provide a by-pass route for Highway 30 when the St. Johns Bridge opened in 1931.

Portland: Three men, Asa Lovejoy, William Overton and Francis Pettygrove, are generally recognized as the founders of the City of Portland. In 1843, Overton, with the help of his partner, Oregon City lawyer Asa Lovejoy, filed a claim for a "clearing" on the west bank of the Willamette River that was destined to become the heart of the city. Overton soon sold his interest to Pettygrove, an Oregon City merchant, for $50.00. Lovejoy and Pettygrove hired a surveyor to establish the lines for a 16-block town. Pettygrove gave the town site his choice for its name, Portland, after winning a coin toss with Lovejoy, who would have named it Boston. In 1845, Lovejoy sold his one-half interest to Benjamin Stark and headed for California, a move that may have been fortuitous, as the big gold strike came shortly thereafter. Pettygrove built a store and wharf at the foot of what became Washington Street. When Pettygrove, General Stephen Coffin and others heard of a plan by St. Helens merchants to build a road from St. Helens to the Tualatin Plains, the Portlanders quickly undertook the construction of a wagon road across the west hills to reach the valley to thwart their competitors plans. This route, which encouraged valley residents to market their products in Portland, became known as Canyon Road. Pettygrove and others also started selling lots in the city.

Early merchants in Portland benefited greatly from the trade generated by the 1849 California gold rush. The city, similarly to other ports along the Columbia River, started shipping lumber, leather, foodstuffs, tools and other items to San Francisco, sparked by the near insatiable demand for goods by the argonauts. A Portland tanner, Daniel Lownsdale, who had established his shop in Portland in 1846, was among the merchants who grew wealthy from this trade. Because of its location at the confluence of the Willamette and Columbia Rivers, Portland soon became a center of commerce and the city grew rapidly. Lot Whitcomb, S.S. White and Berryman Jennings, owners of the Milwaukie townsite, decided to build a steamer, the second such effort in Oregon. The owners brought Jacob Kamm, lately of California, but who had trained as an engineer on the Mississippi, to Oregon to supervise the construction of the steamer. The owners also convinced Captain J.C. Ainsworth to come to Oregon to captain of the new vessel. Ainsworth, who learned the mariner trade on the Mississippi, had also traveled west to California because of the gold rush. He shelved his plan to pilot a steamer on the Sacramento

River when offered the captaincy on the newly christened *Lot Whitcomb*. After the launch, Kamm became its engineer, thus bringing together two men who would later have a profound effect on the transportation industry in the region. In 1854, Kamm built *Jennie Clark*, of which he retained one-half ownership. Ainsworth, George Abernathy and Hiram Clark owned the other one-half. Kamm also superintended the construction of *Carrie Ladd*, which, given his ownership share, secured for him a major ownership position when the Union Transportation Company (UTC) formed. The UTC turned out to be a precursor of the Oregon Steam Navigation Company (OSN). Kamm and R.R. Thompson became the largest stockholders of the OSN upon its incorporation.

William S. Ladd, with the others mentioned above, also helped organize the OSN. Ladd came to Portland from San Francisco in 1852. He first became a partner with Charles E. Tilton in a store. Later the two established the Ladd & Tilton Bank, Portland's first. The bank prospered and Ladd became a major participant in Portland's business community. In addition to the OSN, Ladd helped organize the Oregon Iron and Steel Company and became active in Portland's milling industry, owning mills, at one point, responsible for about 75% of Portland's flour production. Ladd hired Simeon G. Reed, who came to Oregon in 1853, as a clerk. In 1858, Reed purchased an interest in three steamers, *Senorita*, *Belle* and *Multnomah*. Reed, with the other incorporators mentioned above, became a principal in the OSN. Named vice-president of the corporation, he remained in that capacity until Henry Villard took over the firm in 1879. During his tenure, the directors built the portage railways at the Cascades and The Dalles, put in the first telegraph line through the Gorge and purchased the Walla Walla and Columbia River Railroad, which ran from Wallula to Walla Walla. Reed also served as president of the Oregon Iron and Steel Company and held an interest in an Idaho mine as well as other business ventures. Upon his death, Reed bequeathed funds to purchase property and construct buildings for a college campus, which college (Reed College) now bears his name.

Another mariner, Captain John H. Couch, did much to promote Portland as a port. He took up a claim adjacent to that of Lovejoy and Pettygrove. Captain of the bark, *Chenamus*, Couch had many contacts with the seafaring community in Massachusetts and encouraged his friends to dock their ships at Portland. Couch Street honors the captain, who was among those who pioneered the shipment of salted salmon to eastern markets. Several other early pioneers gave their names to streets or districts. Edward J. Northrup, who entered the hardware business, is memorialized by Northrup Street; Philip A. Marquam, who served as a Multnomah County judge (Marquam Hill and the Marquam Bridge); John L. Morrison, merchant (the Morrison bridge and a street); Captain William Irving, active in the steamboat business (the Irvington district); Stephen G. Skidmore, druggist who bequeathed money for the library, for the Congregational Church and for a fountain on First Avenue (Skidmore Fountain and a street). Other place or street names honored early settlers. Lents district in S.E. Portland bears the name of O.P. Lents, who owned a farm in that area. St. Johns took its name from James John, who operated a ferry service from North Portland across the Columbia River to the Washington shore. (Being somewhat of a recluse, he was often called St. John, hence the name.) James Terwilliger, who came to Oregon in 1845, is memorialized by Terwilliger Park and Terwilliger Boulevard. David Burnside gave his name to the bridge and to the street.

In 1854, a shipment of lumber left Portland bound for Hong Kong. A year later, the brig, *Metropolis*, carried the first known shipment of flour to the same destination. Thereafter, shipments of lumber, wheat and flour increased, both to California, the orient and Europe. In 1868, the bark, *Jennie Alice,* berthed in Portland carrying 430 Chinese immigrants, most of whom were soon engaged as laborers clearing land, canning salmon, washing clothes or grading roads. With them came Chinese merchants who imported goods from China to supply the needs of these immigrants, whose numbers increased year by year. This contrubuted to an increase in trade with China as these merchants became involved in the export trade as well as the import trade. Captain J.C. Ainsworth, of the Oregon Steam Navigation Company, had three ships, *Alden Besse*, *Coloma* and *Kate Davenport*, involved in the China trade. T.B. Wilcox built up an immense flour trade to the orient. W.D. Wheelwright shipped lumber all over the world from Portland, helping establish the city as a leading port on the West Coast. T.M. Stevens & Company, Balfour Guthrie & Company, Kerr, Gifford & Company, Portland Flouring Mills and Dant and Russell were among the firms that became established during this era.

In 1850, T.J. Dryer established a weekly newspaper, *The Oregonian*, which Henry L. Pittock purchased in 1860. Henry Corbett, who made a fortune in Portland, opened his general mercantile store in 1851. In 1887, the new Morrison Bridge spanned the Willamette, making the east bank of the river far more accessible. The Steel Bridge, with its lower deck for trains, came in 1888, followed by the Hawthorne Bridge in 1891, the Burnside Bridge in 1894, the Broadway Bridge in 1913, the Sellwood Bridge in 1925 and the Ross Island Bridge in 1926. (The original Morrison, Steel, Hawthorne and Burnside bridges have been replaced.) Between 1885 and 1895, 161 miles of streetcar rails were laid in the city, which came under the control of the Portland Railway Light and Power Company. Its suburban division had lines to Troutdale, Gresham, Boring, Bull Run, Estacada and Oregon City. By 1910, the near monopoly system carried a daily average of 45,000 passengers and its streetcars made an approximate 1000 crossings over Willamette bridges each day. James Hill's Oregon Electric Company lines served Beaverton, Hillsboro, Forest Grove, Tualatin, Wilsonville, Salem and Eugene. The Southern Pacific's "Red Electrics" ran to Garden Home, Beaverton and Hillsboro before swinging south to reach McMinnville and Corvallis. In 1891, the Oregon Legislature created the Port of Portland, giving it the responsibility for maintaining and improving harbor facilities, deepening and maintaining river channels and operating a dry dock for ship repair. Shortly after the turn of the century, the U.S. Army Corps of Engineers deepened the river channel from Portland to Astoria, making it possible for larger ships to reach the Portland harbor.

In 1905, Portland celebrated a historic centennial by sponsoring the Lewis and Clark Exposition, the 100th anniversary of the explorers' trek down the Columbia River. The city hosted 1.6 million visitors for the event, which, with the developments cited above, created such a boom both in business and transportation that by 1910, Portland's population passed 200,000. In 1913, the dynamic spirit generated by the city's growth led its business and political leaders to support the construction of a highway through the Columbia River Gorge. By that year, when construction of the Multnomah County section of the highway commenced, Portland's population had reached 225,000, with two-thirds living in the "eastside" communities of East Portland, Albina, St. Johns, Mt. Tabor, Montavilla, Rose City Park, Woodstock, Eastmoreland and Mt. Scott.

In 1805, Lewis and Clark had missed the Willamette River on their journey down the Columbia. On March 31, 1806, the homeward bound expedition camped on the north bank of the Columbia across from the "Quicksand" [Sandy] River. There they remained for several days. After being informed by the natives that a large river flowed into the Columbia downstream, Captain Clark led a small party to explore its lower reaches. The leaders had earlier decided that "there must be some other considerable river which flowed into the Columbia on its south side below us which we have not yet seen, as the extensive valley on that side of the river lying between the mountainous country of the Coast [Range] and the Western [Cascade] mountains must be watered by some stream." Thus, Captain Clark ventured into the "Multnomah" [Willamette] River. He ascended about five miles up the river, thus passing the future site of the city of Portland.

54

Lewis and Clark Exposition And Oriental Fair, Portland, 1905

Top: The Exposition grounds with Mt. Hood in the distance, Union Station, center right. The domed structure (center-left) is the Palace of Agriculture. Middle: The Forestry Building, which was the Lewis and Clark Memorial for the exposition. Bottom (left): The "Trail" or entrance to the Exposition, which referenced the "trail" that the explorers took from St. Louis to reach the Columbia River and the Pacific Ocean. Photo postcards, the author.

City of Portland

Downtown Portland from the Hawthorne Bridge.   *Photo postcards, the author.*

Spanning the Willamette River

The "New" Broadway Bridge, 1913.   *Photo postcard, the author.*

56

U.S. Courthouse

ngregational Church, Portland, Oregon.

Washington Street

Congregational Church, Portland

57

Corbett Building

Wells Fargo Building

3rd Street, Downtown Portland.

Benson Hotel. (A.E. Doyle, architect)

Portland - Seaport

11 storage tanks for vegetable oil and molasses, Northwest Industrial Area (ca 1920).
Photos courtesy of George Perry VI.

Portland's Lumber Trade

Peninsula Lumber Company, Portland ca 1920

Shipping Terminal

Terminal 4, Portland, Oregon ca 1920.   *Photo courtesy of George Perry VI.*

Train Station

Portland's Union Depot, built in the 1890s.   *Photo postcard (1908), the author.*

Downtown Portland

Left: Fifth Avenue with the Meier & Frank and Lipman Wolfe Stores on the left. Meier & Frank, founded in 1857, became Portland's most noted department store. The Meier and Frank store shown, completed in three phases (1909, 1915, 1932) was among a group of Portland's first skyscrapers.

Photo courtesy of Steve Lehl.

Below: A route man for Portland's Yuan Dairy delivers milk to customers. Yuan's Dairy was located on Columbia Boulevard.

1913 photo, Laura Mershon.

Yuan's Dairy, Portland

Portland, City of Roses

A rose hedge encloses the yard of this S.W. Portland home ca 1920.

Mt. Hood From Portland

Portland's population in 1920 was 258,288.   *Photos courtesy of George Perry VI.*

East Multnomah County, Fairview and Troutdale

Enthusiasts were proposing a road through the Gorge soon after the automobile appeared on roads. A "Good Roads" group, composed of John S. Beall, E.F. Cannon, C.S. Jackson (*Oregon Journal*), Frank C. Riggs (Packard Motors) and E. Henry Wemme (Willamette Tent and Awning [later White Stag]), proposed both the improvement of existing roads and new construction. On April 11, 1911, the *Gresham Outlook* headlined, "Portland-Hood River Highway Proposed." The article quoted Judge Cleeton: "From a scenic standpoint it is almost impossible to conceive of a more picturesque [highway] than that from Bridal Veil up the great Columbia River [Gorge] into the city of Hood River." The estimated cost was $100,000. In the spring of 1913, a number of "road improvement clubs," including the "East Multnomah County Road Improvement Club" were formed to push for a proposed highway through the Gorge.

Bonds issued by Multnomah County permitted the start of construction during the summer of 1913. Many local farmers responded to a call from Charlie Bramhall, road boss, for workers to help with the construction. Initially, a farmer working with his own team pulling a Fresno, wagon or grader earned $4.50 per 10 hour day; laborers received $2.25. In 1914, the county increased the daily rates to $5.00 [team] and $2.50 [laborer]. That fall, the *Outlook* quoted John B. Yeon, newly appointed Multnomah County Roadmaster, as favoring a new road from Troutdale along the Sandy River "to the [Nielson] bridge at the automobile club's resort." (The bridge was named after Carl C. Nielson, an early settler on the Sandy River.) The county considered that the Columbia River Highway (CRH) commenced at the northern end of the Nielson bridge. In January, 1914, county commissioners decided to make improvements to both Baseline Road (Stark) and the road from Troutdale to the Nielson Bridge in order to connect the Sandy Road to the CRH. On April 25, 1914, a truck loaded with gravel caused the Nielson Bridge to collapse, sending the load and five men into the Sandy River. Roadboss Charlie

John B. Yeon, Roadmaster

Yeon directed the road bosses, who supervised the crews who worked to build the highway.   *Photo courtesy of ODOT.*

Bramhall suffered a broken arm in the mishap, but, according to the *Outlook*, the other four (including the author's father, George Mershon) suffered only "a cold dip in the river." The county completed a replacement steel bridge that same year. By October, 1914, construction of the segment between the bridges was underway. In November, commissioners proposed a bond issue to pave the Sandy River section (8.6 miles) from the Troutdale Bridge to the highway and to pave the Columbia River Highway to the county line (20.5 miles).

Because of the number of dairy farms located along Sandy Road from Eighty-Second Avenue east, Sandy had become known as "dairy row." Early settlers included Jacob Zimmerman, who established a herd of Brown Swiss cattle; Wencel Schantin, a mixed herd; John Hall, a Holstein herd; William Tegart, who also had Holsteins; and Jacob Luscher, another dairy farmer with Holsteins. Fairview Farms, owned by the Eckelman family, had a herd of Guernsey cows. The Eckelmans, who operated many milk routes, also purchased milk and cream from other dairy farmers. In 1926, as mentioned earlier, Multnomah County improved Sandy Road from the Portland city limits to the Gresham-Fairview Road (now 223rd Avenue). In 1926, Congress passed the proposed national highway standards. In the 1927-28 biennium, Oregon adopted them. At that time, Sandy Road (later, Sandy Boulevard) officially became part of U.S. Oregon Highway 30, the designation for the Columbia River Highway.

Fairview: Completing an overland journey by covered wagon on the Oregon Trail, the Addison C. Dunbar family of seven arrived at the mouth of the Sandy River in November, 1850. Mr. Dunbar, with his wife, Hester A. (Zumwalt) Dunbar, filed for a donation land claim of 640 acres, which included land in what later became the town of Fairview. Another early settler, John P. Heslin, married Drusilla Dunbar, a union that influenced the history of Fairview greatly. Other early settlers included Dr. John Crosby, the Swank family, the Hiram and Bert Stone families, S.A. Arata, C.M. La Follette, the Zimmerman family and the Cree family. (Fairview Village, the former Multnomah Kennel Club and more recent developments are now found on the former Stone farm.) When the Yakima Indian War erupted in 1856, Chief John (aka "Indian John"), leader of a band of the Multnomah tribe who formerly lived in the area, warned settlers living west of the Sandy River of the danger.

Indian John's tribe had been decimated by epidemics of smallpox, measles and other communicable diseases caught from early traders. According to stories repeated by descendants of early settlers, his band had also suffered a catastrophic loss when an overhanging cliff face (part of Broughton Bluff) gave way suddenly and buried his people's camp. According to the story, the slide took the remainder of his small band, leaving Indian John and his wife the sole survivors. When Indian John's wife died, he laid her to rest among the native dead at an island up the Columbia River. Indian John lived in a log cabin on the Zimmerman place. He performed odd jobs for settlers, such as tanning hides and tending their livestock. He called on his neighbors and certainly knew the Dunbar and Heslin families.

In 1881, Addison C. Dunbar's heirs quitclaimed the balance of the family's holdings to John P. and Drusilla Heslin. In the 1890s, Edd Heslin acquired more than 100 acres that his uncle, John Dunbar, had owned until he died of tuberculosis. In 1903, Heslin sold this acreage to John Townsend. The Townsend farm remained in the family until sold for commercial development almost exactly one-hundred years later. In 1909, John P. and Drusilla Heslin divided the remainder of the former Dunbar property among their six children. Edward "Edd," who had the first choice, took an approximate 20-acre parcel that stretched south from Bridge Street to the Pacific Railway interurban line (Halsey Street). Mary C. "Calla" received an adjacent parcel to the east. (Calla attended the teachers' college at Monmouth, became a school teacher and taught school until she retired.) John obtained an L-shaped parcel west of Edd's land. Claude received about 10 acres lying along Fairview Creek that included the new home built by his father. Claude had lost his first wife, Jennie Steele, in an accident. He and his second wife, Stella Blair, operated a small fruit stand near Fairview Creek for years. Ethel and Hester "Anna" were deeded parcels south of the interurban line. Ethel's property was located at the S.E. corner where Duck Lane (Fairview Avenue) intersected the Pacific Railway interurban line (Halsey Street). Anna also taught school, which profession she continued after her marriage to Joseph W. "Warren" Heiny

Fairview, platted in 1889, became an incorporated town in 1908. By 1905, Edd Heslin and his wife, Helen M. (Littlepage) Heslin, had moved to a home located at 60 Main Street. Edd Heslin served on the first city council, a position he held for sixteen years. He became mayor in

1924, and served 13 years in that office. In 1912, Fairview completed its first city hall. Commercial enterprises in Fairview included Frank Axtell's cheese factory (that later became a store) and his "hall," which was used for community events. Mr. Cree owned a store and a blacksmith shop. He also worked as a carpenter, building many structures in Fairview and Troutdale. The Oregon Railroad and Navigation Company (OR & N.) established a station in Fairview in 1882. Since a postoffice in Coos County carried the "Fairview" name, the local office required a different designation. Milton Hosford proposed "Cleone," which was adopted. However, the OR & N. depot retained its "Fairview" designation. The Pacific Railway Company interurban line came to Fairview in 1906, and a year later, reached Troutdale. From Fairview, the interurban line ran west to a point just beyond the (present) 201st Avenue where it turned south, crossed Baseline (Stark), the Mount Hood Division line and continued south to Linnemann Junction near Cedarville. There, it intercepted the Springwater interurban line that connected Portland with Gresham, Boring, Eagle Creek and Estacada. The interurban lines suspended operations in 1927. After the "Fairview" postoffice in Coos County closed in 1913, "Cleone" officially became "Fairview" a year later. The 1911 graduates of Fairview School were: Lloyd Anderson, Henry Moller, Guy Bennett, Carl Heslin, Lillian Copeland, Harry Gustafson, Winifred Bennett and Maurice Schram (son of the postmaster).

Troutdale: Lt. William R. Broughton, in an armed tender, *Chatham*, explored the lower reaches of the Columbia River in 1792, reaching a point above what is now the Sandy River. Broughton Bluff is named for the explorer, who was a member of Captain George Vancouver's English expedition. Lewis and Clark, who camped on the north shore of the Columbia, explored the lower reaches of the Sandy River in November, 1805, as they descended the Columbia on their way to the sea. The explorers noted, "...this river throws out emence quantitys of sand and is very shallow..." They named it the "Quicksand River" because of this accumulation of sand, apparently volcanic ash from a recent eruption of Mt. Hood. Indian John's story is given some credence by the number of artifacts found by road crews constructing the highway, which included a carved stone "turtle" recovered by roadboss Charlie Bramhall in 1914. An Indian trail, later designated the "wire trail," used by early settlers to bring their cattle from The Dalles to the Willamette Valley, crossed the Sandy River near the present Troutdale Bridge. From the south bank, the trail wound its way up the bluff to reach the plateau above Troutdale, then continued on to the falls of the Willamette at Oregon City.

According to writer Sharon Nesbit, the earliest settlers to file land claims in the area included John Douglass, David F. Buxton, Benjamin Hall, James M. Stott and Felix B. Hicklin. Buxton, with his wife, Fannie, is credited by Troutdale historians as being the first settler in what is now downtown Troutdale. He donated land for a school and established the town's first water supply. Hicklin filed his 320-acre claim on the east bank of the Sandy River, where he established a dairy herd. Reputedly, he built the first dwelling east of the Sandy River in Multnomah County (see p. 70). He eventually accumulated more than 1100 acres on the delta of the Sandy River. Establishment of the town, however, awaited the arrival of Captain John Harlow, a former sea captain and prominent Portland businessman. Harlow purchased part of the Buxton claim and, by 1872, had built a country home. Harlow put in a number of fish ponds; accordingly, he named his farm, Troutdale. Harlow used his influence to convince the OR & N to build a depot close to where its rail line crossed the Sandy River. The company named its depot, Troutdale, after the captain's farm. After Harlow's death, his widow, Celestia Harlow, following her husband's instructions, platted the town. In 1891, the town had a restaurant (the Ellis), a meat market (Kannath and Redding), Kelly & Stephenson's mercantile, Doddridge and Tracy's hardware, a real estate office and Aaron Fox's store, which he had purchased that year. In the early 1890s, the Union Meat Company built a plant in Troutdale. A Troutdale teacher, Glenora

Emily, met and married Jack Vandeveer, a carpenter employed in building the structure. John Sweeney, Justice of the Peace at Latourell, performed the ceremony. While Vandeveer worked helping build the packing plant, Glenora ran a boarding house and gave art lessons.

In 1907, Troutdale became an incorporated city. Improvements came rapidly. In 1911, the city granted Mt. Hood Railway & Power Company a 50-year franchise for "light, heat and power" (*Outlook*). In May, 1911, the O W R & N. (formerly the OR & N - see "Notes," p. 263) completed a new railroad bridge across the Sandy River. In February, 1912, Multnomah County dynamited the wood highway bridge across the Sandy River. The county replaced the structure with a steel bridge that same year. In July, the *Outlook* reported: "Mt. Hood Railway & Power Company has erected poles and strung wires into Troutdale," which brought electricity to the town.

Because of its location on the Sandy River and because of its depot on the OR & N line, Troutdale became an important shipping center for railroad ties and farm produce. Mills in the hinterlands along the Sandy River used the annual spring freshet to launch thousands of ties in "tie drives" to Troutdale. The ties, upon reaching slack water at Troutdale, were held by booms, retrieved, stacked and shipped by rail to supply railroad construction projects underway across the country. The tie drive of 1913 ended the practice as Troutdale's Davenport Milling Company decided that ties could more easily be hauled out by truck. Horace McGinnis moved to Troutdale from Michigan early in the century. He had grown celery in Michigan, and recognized the river bottomland here as ideal for growing celery, which crop he introduced in 1907. By 1912, several growers were involved, including C.S. Wilson, Simoni & Company, Thomas Kuge and T. Morashita. On August 2, 1912, the *Gresham Outlook* reported that the first carload of celery had been shipped from Troutdale by McGinnis. In 1923, celery grown by Troutdale farmers Morris McGinnis, Clarence Parsons, Jim Spence and others garnered first place in the "Celery King" contest held in Buffalo, New York. In 1925, local growers shipped more than 100 carloads of prize-winning celery from Troutdale, the self-proclaimed "Celery Capital of the World."

In May, 1911, A.C. Coltman, an English prune buyer, came to east Multnomah County on an inspection trip. He stated (*Outlook*), "Oregon prunes are the finest in the world. They are richer in flavor and substance than California prunes and [are even] better than the famous prunes of France. The demand in England is increasing daily." Another buyer, William Ellison, bought local prunes to ship east. In September, the *Outlook* reported, "A large number of carloads [of prunes] have been shipped east and to local markets and work is still going on. The shipments average two carloads a day. Quite a force of workmen are required in handling the business." (The prune industry ended with a severe ice storm that hit east Multnomah County on November 19, 1921, which destroyed the local Italian Prune orchards.) The *Outlook* continued to report produce shipments from Troutdale. On June 21, 1912: "Nearly 1 thousand crates of strawberries were shipped from Troutdale by the Troutdale Produce and Fruit Grower's Association and Blazer Fruit company." On October 17, 1913, this appeared: "A.D. Mershon (the author's grandfather) shipped a carload of cabbage to Puget Sound, the first car shipped this season." On October 28, a follow-up article: "A.D. Mershon shipped his third car [of cabbage] to Los Angeles." Thus, before the highway came through, Troutdale had become a major shipping terminal for growers in the surrounding area.

Shortly after the end of World War I, Ernest F. Peterson obtained cauliflower seed from Denmark, built up a stock of seed and introduced the crop to Troutdale farmers. He, George Chamberlain, W.E. Hurt, W.J. Jackson, Frank Fehrenbacher and others formed the Troutdale Lettuce and Cauliflower Growers' Association. In 1923, the *Outlook* reported that the association expected to ship 50 carloads of cauliflower and 15-20 carloads of lettuce. In 1925, the association shipped more than 200 carloads of cauliflower and lettuce. M.B. McKay, former professor at Oregon Agricultural College (now Oregon State University) founded the Troutdale Potato Growers' Association. The association developed a market for certified seed potatoes. California potato growers became the principal outlet for the association's disease-free stock, grown on local farms. Within three decades, Troutdale had become an extremely important marketing center for local farmers. Celery, prunes, berries, cabbage, cauliflower, lettuce, potatoes and carrots, packed and shipped by rail across the country, supported the agricultural economy of East Multnomah County. In 1929, with few exceptions, these organized groups faded into oblivion with the onset of the "great depression." Actually, it hit local farmers in 1928 when the cauliflower association failed to pay many of its members for produce shipped that year.

When the highway came through, Aaron Fox still had a store in Troutdale. John Larsson operated a saloon and a livery stable. (His wife, Clara [Latourell] Larsson, served as Mayor.) The Tiller Hotel and Café offered lodging and meals. F.E. Harlow managed a restaurant and hotel in the Reinhardt Building. Z.S. Shantz owned and operated the Model Meat Market. Three individuals, William Wiser, George Pleasant and James Cook, built garages to serve motorists using the new highway. (Ivan "Ike" Handy purchased the former Wiser garage after World War II.) In the 1920s, Tad Johnson put up a hot dog stand at the north end of the Troutdale Bridge, which became popular with farmers and smelt fishermen. By the late '20s, the stand had become Tad's Tap Pot Inn. In 1947, because a connecting road required the property, the restaurant changed hands and location. Tad's is now owned by Judy Jones, whose family has owned and operated Tad's for more than 50 years.

Approaching Fairview

CRH near Fairview (Mt. Hood in background) ca 1920.

Photo courtesy of George Perry VI.

Railway Underpass, Approach To Troutdale

The CRH passes beneath the O W R & N tracks near Troutdale.   Photo courtesy of ODOT

Troutdale ca 1890

An early (ca 1890) photograph of Troutdale. (The white building at the base of the street lies beyond the railroad tracks [see next page]).   *Photos courtesy of the Woodard family.*

Railroad Station, Troutdale

Oregon Railroad and Navigation Company Steam engine at the Troutdale station. The water tower visible in the photo on the preceding page stands behind the train.

Hicklin Ferry at Troutdale ca 1902

The Hicklin Ferry slip, just north of the Hicklin home, appears in the photo of the Hicklin farm on the next page. The delivery wagon reputedly belongs to Aaron Fox, who had a mercantile store in Troutdale.   *Photo courtesy of Stephanie Rickert.*

F.G. Hicklin Farm, Troutdale

F.G. Hicklin took a 360-acre donation land claim here, then added acreage until he had accumulated an approximate 1,100 acres, which he used for a dairy. The home was reputedly the first home east of the Sandy River in Multnomah County, located under Broughton Bluff along the Sandy River (next page, also).   *Photo courtesy of the Woodard Family.*

OR & N Depot, Troutdale

The OR & N's first depot in Troutdale was a two-story structure in which the station agent, A.D. Kendall, lived (upper level). The depot burned in the 1907 fire.

Photo courtesy of the Woodard Family.

Tie Drives, Destination Troutdale

Top left: Mills along the Sandy River, such as the Bramhall, the Kelly and Wihlon and the Cameron Hogg mills filled the Sandy River with ties during the spring freshet. Top right, from left: Tom Northway, Arnie Rickert and Bill Northway "ride" the ties to Troutdale, breaking up jams and recovering ties that hang-up on the river bank. Though a thrill, it was dangerous work and some men inevitably lost their lives. Below: Ties are corraled at Troutdale.

Photos courtesy of Lorraine (Wright) Scott (1 & 3) and Bob Van Speybrock (2).

The Troutdale Bridge, Built in 1912

The Troutdale Bridge during smelt runs. Right: The Wire Trail descended to the river through the gap, far right.   *Photos courtesy of Lorraine (Wright) Scott and Dave Wand, respectively.*

Ogden Farm, Troutdale

This photo, taken from a point on Woodard Road, is a view looking towards the mouth of the Sandy River. The highway skirted Broughton Bluff (right), and followed the Sandy River to the "upper" (Stark Street) bridge   . Photo courtesy of Dorothy Hungerford.

Multnomah County Crusher, Columbia River Highway Project

Rock Crusher, Columbia River Highway along the Sandy River, ca 1913.

Photo courtesy of Lorraine (Wright) Scott.

Troutdale Family Takes a Tour ca 1916

Joachim and Elsa Suhr take their children, Alice and Arthur, for a ride on the newly paved Baseline Road (Stark Street), one of two roads that accessed the new Columbia River Highway.
Photos courtesy of Dave Wand.

Camping Trip ca 1919

Oregon's new highway system provided access to campgrounds and newly established parks, to which these young Troutdale residents are bound. From left (back), (believed to be [btb]) Lizzie Seidl, [btb] Dorothy Kendall, returning veteran Alex Lampert, Opal Monahan, [btb] Olive Parsons, Evelyn Kendall, returning veteran Julius "Jack" Lampert and Arnold Lampert. Middle: Emma Lampert. Front, Clarence Parsons, Ferd Lampert (driving), [btb] Marguerite Kendall, Bessie Low, Agnes Seidl, unknown [hidden], Cab Seidl, Merle Monahan, (unknown [hidden]), Barney Woodard and Herman Blazer. Standing: unidentified [may be Jesse Coons] .

12-Mile Roadhouse

12-Mile Roadhouse, located on Stark Street, an "access route" to the Columbia River Highway ca 1914. *Photo courtesy of Rosetta Henkle.*

Grading the New Columbia River Highway

Road Grader, Columbia River Highway ca 1914 (near Stark Street Bridge).
Photo courtesy of Lorraine (Wright) Scott.

East Multnomah County, Springdale and Corbett

The highway: From the Nielson bridge, the highway began a gradual ascent to reach Chanticleer Point (at 925 feet above the river). It passed through the hamlets of Springdale and Corbett. In 1915, with work progressing rapidly on the new highway, many projects were underway in Springdale. According to the *Gresham Outlook* (March 30, 1915), Harley Bates and Fred Salzman had "lumber on the ground and will commence building [a new garage]." By May, 1915, work on the highway had progressed through Springdale and was proceeding on "the section between Springdale and [Ivo] Van Speybrock's [place]." By June, in addition to William W. Northway's store and John B. True's store and creamery (owned by Raleigh True after his father's death in March), Springdale had the new Bates-Salzman garage. An *Outlook* reporter wrote, "Harley Bates and Fred Salzman, who own a new garage at Springdale, are busy all the time."

Meanwhile, work on the new sections of the highway continued. By October 8, 1915, the *Outlook* speculated that "the road being built along the east side of the Sandy River between the two bridges will probably be ready for travel this year." By the end of October, the Warren Company had completed the paving of the highway from the new Stark Street Bridge to a point beyond Multnomah Falls. In December, Road boss Charlie Bramhall and farmer Will Henkle toured the highway by automobile, doubtless to see the result of theirs' (and others') hard work. In November, 1915, an extension of Baseline Road to the new bridge (Stark Street) was authorized, culminating a six-year effort that created much controversy. On April 14, 1916, the paper reported that the Warren Company was "paving the Baseline [Stark Street] extension" as well as the "connecting link" between the Troutdale and Stark Street bridges. Consequently, by the spring of 1916, East Multnomah County residents had a much improved, paved highway into Troutdale as well as major improvements to Stark Street that provided more direct access to Gresham and Southeast Portland.

Corbett: At the time the Gorge highway was proposed, Corbett (hereafter, Lower Corbett) had a railroad station, a landing for fishermen and steamboats, a telephone office and a couple of stores. The town was situated on the south bank of the Columbia River and on the Oregon-Washington Railroad and Navigation Company rail line. Upper Corbett, located on the Wire Trail, had no commercial establishments, but did have a grade school (Taylor) and the Corbett Community Church (under construction). The "Wire Trail," a trail used by Native Americans for trade between Celilo Falls and the falls on the Willamette, was used by the telegraph company as a right-of-way when it ran its line from Portland east in 1868. After Walter Knight, who owned a store in Lower Corbett, learned that the highway was to be built through Upper Corbett (hereafter, Corbett), he immediately purchased land along the route of the new highway and proceeded to build a store there. Later, he added a garage and a dance hall.

In 1885, former U.S. Senator Henry W. Corbett obtained a section of land that had been homesteaded by E.F. Taylor. Senator Corbett, who had earned a fortune in the mercantile business in the bustling town of Portland, built a palatial summer home on the property, which he used until his death in 1903 (the home burned in 1922). Senator Corbett had platted his holdings in Corbett and, after the new highway came through, his heirs disposed of plots of the estate, which included properties both north and south of the highway. Much of the development that took place in Corbett occurred on land formerly part of the Senator's estate, including the site for the new Union High School, Columbian High (CHS). CHS opened its doors to students in September, 1915.

Since the highway through Corbett followed the ancient Wire Trail, less clearing and grading were required except for a cut-off near the grange hall. On April 6, 1915, grange patrons passed a resolution supporting the $1,250,000 bond issue to pay for paving the highway. Multnomah County voters approved the measure and by August, 1915, the highway was paved through Corbett as far as Knight's Grocery. Farmers, using teams and wagons, hauled the Warrenite (hot stuff) from the Company's "batch plant," located across the highway from the new high school, to the work site. There, the material was spread, then packed with a steamroller.

Developments proceeded apace. On March 8, 1914, Pastor Reeder dedicated the Corbett Community Church. In July, 1915, Walter Knight opened his new store and dance hall situated just east of the new high school. George Chamberlain, who owned a store on Evans Road, sold his property to J. Ward Evans. He purchased eleven acres on the new highway and opened a new store in July, 1917. He soon added a camground and an auto court. Chamberlain's original store is now owned and operated by Susan Leigh as the Corbett Country Market. The Chamberlain home, adjacent to the store, is now operated as a bed and breakfast by Chamberlain's granddaughter, Nancy Wilson.

In December, 1917, Columbia Telephone Company relocated its exchange into a newly constructed headquarters building near Chamberlain's store in Corbett. Frank Bell purchased a couple of lots from Chamberlain and opened a new garage for business in November, 1919. When Knight's business complex caught fire on July 3, 1922, destroying it and the adjacent high school, Knight's garage manager, Harry Rickert, purchased a site across the highway to the west and built a new garage. Later, he expanded the business by adding a café. After the high school burned, Union High School District #1 built a new high school west of its former site, which opened for students in September, 1923. Also in 1923, Roy Andersen and Clarence Bush opened a store across the highway from the new school. In 1925, Claude Woodle opened a hardware store adjacent to Andersen and Bush's establishment. Thus, within ten years, the town of Corbett, once centered on the river, was now situated about one-mile south on the new highway. Farmers, who previously shipped their products by rail or sternwheeler from Lower Corbett could now transport their farm produce to Portland by truck.

East Multnomah County - Between Troutdale and Bridal Veil

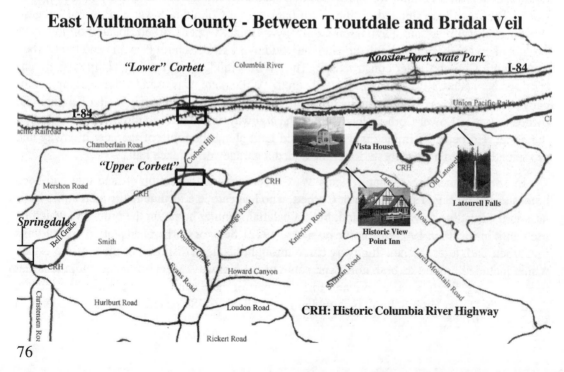

Roadboss Charlie Bramhall and Family

Charlie Bramhall suffered this broken arm when the Nielson Bridge across the Sandy River collapsed. His family: son, Lloyd, wife, Alma and son, Kenneth.   Photo, Pat (Bramhall) Paget.

The Stark Street Bridge, 1916

The Stark Street Bridge, completed in 1914. (Note: The extension of the highway between the upper and lower bridges is under construction.) This extension required the removal of the standard arch rail approaches seen.   Photo postcard courtesy of Steve Lehl.

Dabney Park on the Sandy River

The original Dabney Park, Sandy River. *Photo courtesy of Micheal Gibbons.*

Road Crew, Columbia River Highway Near Springdale, 1914

Gene Berney holds the team on the left, Tom Northway, the team on right; George Mershon and Louis Nielson kneel in front of the team on right. (Others not known.) *Photo, the author.*

Roy Parson's Garage, Springdale

While Fred Salzman was in the army during World War I, Roy Parsons managed Salzman's garage. When Salzman returned from the service, Parsons opened his own garage a couple of blocks west. Edna Parsons dispensed gigantic ice cream cones, five cents each, in her little shop that customers entered through the door on the left (front).   Photo, Bob Wenzel.

Salzman Brothers Business Complex, Springdale

Fred and William Salzman's garage, confectionary, barber shop, hotel and auto camp in the late 1920s.   *Photo courtesy of Steve Gillmer.*

William Northway Works on the Highway

William Northway used his teams to pull this grader, which was used in the construction of the highway. He also owned a store in Springdale.   *Photos courtesy of Bob Wenzel.*

Highway Construction in Springdale, 1914

Farmers using teams pulling Fresnos form and level the highway roadbed through Springdale.
Photo courtesy of Lorraine (Wright) Scott.

Springdale Garage, Market and Hotel, ca 1933

"Cook" Christensen (with grandson Mel Christensen), delivers milk to the market in Salzman's complex, Springdale. Compare this depression-era photo with that on the bottom of page 87.
Photo courtesy of Mel Christensen.

The Remodeled Springdale Grade School, 1922

Springdale Grade School, on the Columbia River Highway.   *Photo, the author.*

Springdale Grade School, ca 1938

In remodeling the first school (previous page), the crew removed a bearing wall, which weakened the structure. This replacement was built in 1932.   *Photo courtesy of Rosetta Henkle.*

Woodle's Hardware and Arneson's Store, Corbett, 1930s.

Corbett's Woodle's Hardware (left) and the Bush/Andersen store (right). Columbian High School students (including Marion Kirkham, front) relax on the school lawn.   *Photo, Sandra Gedde.*

Rickert's Garage, Corbett

Rickert's Garage, Corbett, Harry Rickert, proprietor, built in 1922 (the automobile is a Model-T Ford, mid-1920s).   *Photo courtesy of Sandra Gedde.*

Corbett Community Church, Dedicated, 1914

Since the CRH followed the "Wire Trail" through "Upper" Corbett, the church benefitted from the access provided by the highway.   *Photo courtesy of Pat Paget.*

Schools at Corbett, 1915

Corbett (aka Taylor) Grade School (left), built in 1884; Columbian High School, right, built in 1914-15   .   Photo courtesy of Nancy (Roley) Wilson.

W.R. Knight's New Market, Corbett

W.R. Knight's new Corbett store, built in 1915 (later he added a garage). Knight built on the new CRH, selling out in "Lower Corbett."   Photo courtesy of Sandra Gedde.

The Warren Company "Batch" Plant, Corbett, Oregon, 1915

The Warren Company's plant to mix and heat "Warrenite" was located across the new highway from Columbian High School in Corbett. (Note: See photo, top of the previous page.)

Farmer Sam Hulit Hauls "Hot Stuff" to Pave the New Highway

Sam Hulit, farmer, hauling "hot stuff," (Warrenite) for paving the Columbia River Highway (at Corbett).   *Photos, the author.*

Corbett Country Market, Established by George H. Chamberlain

George Chamberlain's store est. 1917; Perry Settlemier (near entry), proprietor, 1923-1958 (Corbett).   *Photo courtesy of Susan Leigh.*

A more recent photograph of Chamberlain's Market, Susan Leigh, Proprietor.
Photo, the author.

East Multnomah County - Columbia Heights

The Columbia Heights section of the Columbia River Highway, for our purposes, starts about one-half mile east of Corbett at Crestview Lane and terminates at Latourell. In March, 1914, the County started the construction of a work camp near the Summit to provide lodging and meals for from 125-150 workers. Laborers earned $2.50 for a ten-hour day and paid 25 cents for camp meals. According to the *Gresham Outlook*, work on the highway was underway by May, 1914, when two local farmers, Roy Andersen and William Ross, had the "honor of moving the first scraper of dirt" for the Heights section. Multnomah County also located a crusher near the Summit to supply gravel for the highway. In this stretch, the western portion followed the Wire Trail to Chanticleer Point, which is 925 feet above sea level. At the point, the "trail" dropped to the riverbank near Rooster Rock. From Chanticleer, the highway curved southeasterly to the Summit, which, at an elevation of slightly more than 1000 feet, is the highest point on the CRH. From the Summit, the next one-half mile is literally blasted from the cliff face. In Samuel Lancaster's words, it "is hung around the tops of the cliffs like the cornice of a tall building." The necessity of blasting took a toll. On September 10, 1914, a rock from a blast near the Summit struck M. Sesigino, an Italian stonemason, killing him instantly. According to local lore, his remains were interred close to the work camp on the ridge above Thor's Point. From the Summit eastward, retaining walls topped either by guard rocks or by standard-arched masonry rails were constructed by these artisans. This stone work became an integral part of Lancaster's plan to build a highway that would endure.

Simon Benson

Simon Benson, lumberman, entrepreneur, visionary planner and philanthropist, led in the effort to build the CRH.

Photo courtesy of David Sell.

The topography from the Summit to Latourell presented Samuel Lancaster with two great challenges: traversing Thor's Point and making the descent from there to Latourell in the limited space available. In 1913, Multnomah County's surveyor asserted that a road through this section could not be built. Lancaster's engineering genius proved him wrong. Lancaster utilized the stone-laying prowess of immigrant Italian stonemasons to circle Thor's Point with a roadway supported by a stone retaining wall. Concrete pillars provide support for a sidewalk along its outer edge. Lancaster reported: "The road almost encircles a high point of rock which stands 700 feet straight up" from the Columbia. "The road fits the top of this rock like the band on your hat, and traverses 225 degrees as it curves on a radius of 110 feet." To complete the descent to Latourell, Lancaster designed a series of majestic loops that dropped the highway close to 700 feet. These loops soon became known as the "Figure Eight." To avoid massive cuts on slide-prone slopes, Lancaster utilized retaining walls to support the highway.

One incident that occurred near the Summit illustrates the contributions of Simon Benson, whose efforts and public-spirited attitude ensured not only that the highway would be built, but that it would be a model to emulate. A recalcitrant landowner, who could not reach a settlement with Multnomah County with regard to the value of his property, posted "no trespassing" signs that effectively stopped construction on the highway at his property line. An account of the meeting held between County officials and the property owner appeared in the *Gresham Outlook,* at which an official stated, "The County can not afford to pay more." In response, Simon Benson "pulled out his pocket book and from there took a hundred-dollar bill, which was added to the sum that the Court allowed and the property owner agreed to let them go." This was one of many such altruistic moves by Benson to keep the project on schedule.

Commercial development at the Heights was quite limited until the highway came through. George and Carrie (Emily) Gill had a store on the Wire Trail near Chanticleer Point. The upstairs served as a dance hall where patrons danced a quadrille, a reel, a polka or a waltz to fiddle music provided by the author's grandfather, James Clarence Wilson. The store served as headquarters for the "Bones and Feather Club," an organization dedicated to stealing poultry after which the culprits invited the victim to a dinner featuring the purloined fowl. Close by, the Chanticleer Inn opened in 1912, a year before construction of the highway commenced. According to accounts, Jim Deaver was so enamored of Madge Kay Morgan that he gave her the property on which the Inn was built. Margaret (Darling) Henderson became a driving force in the opening and operation of the restaurant, for which she served as hostess. Her culinary skills and vibrant personality drew patrons to the establishment, which quickly gained a reputation for excellence. Local farmers earned "side money" pulling motorists out of mud holes. On August 27, 1913, the Multnomah County Commission under Rufus Holman met at the Chanticleer Inn and voted to proceed with the construction of the highway. On August 28, the County hired Samuel Lancaster as consulting engineer for the project, a most fortuitous choice.

Development proceeded apace with construction of the highway. In May, 1914, the Ross family opened a small ice cream parlor at the Summit managed by their daughter, Laura Ross. By May, 1915, Jim Ross had added a gasoline station to the business complex. In June that year, the Rooster Rock Water Company completed a 4-inch line from its spring near Rooster Rock and piped water to Columbia Heights. Water from this spring, piped to storage tanks above Crown Point, provided water for the Vista House and other facilities at the Point. (These tanks are still visible from the highway.) Margaret Henderson (Margaret Hackett by her first marriage), had a falling-out with Alba Morgan, owner of the Chanticleer Inn. She, in some sort of business arrangement with Harold Maffet, built the Falls Chalet at Latourell, which opened in June, 1914. When this establishment burned to the ground in January, 1915, Henderson decided to build her own restaurant. She found a location on the ridge above Crown Point and on May 15, 1915, celebrated the completion of her Crown Point Chalet. The Chalet became an instant success. In December, 1915, the Chalet lost its roof to the east wind, but local farmers soon replaced it. They spoke highly of Margaret Henderson's gracious hospitality during the ordeal. Mrs. Henderson's father, H.L. Darling, a pioneer homesteader in Oregon and prominent wood finisher and cabinetmaker, applied his skill to the interior appointments of the Chalet; its appearance reflected his artistry with wood and his attention to detail. Electricity arrived in August, 1917, leading one observer to write, "the [Chalet] is aglow with electric lights." As the grandeur of the Columbia River Gorge became better known to tourists, the Chalet attracted personalities and celebrities from around the world.

A more accessible Gorge also attracted wealthy Portland businessmen. In 1914, Julius Meier, active in promoting the highway through his leadership of the Columbia River Highway Association, acquired part of John Painter's homestead from the estate's only surviving heir, Sam Painter. Meier had Portland architect A.E. Doyle design a "summer home," which featured a vaulted living room 30-by-46 feet and huge, unpeeled log columns throughout. Unfortunately, the logs provided a perfect home for carpenter ants, termites and other insect pests. Consequently, this mansion had to be replaced by a more lasting structure, which was completed by May, 1927. The Meier family named their estate, Menucha. The First Presbyterian Church, Portland, now owns the estate. In 1917, Edward Ehrman, partner in a wholesale grocery business, constructed a "summer home" west of the Meier estate, also designed by A.E. Doyle. Ehrman named this estate, Ehrmanor, and marked its entrance with a large rectangular basalt boulder emblazoned by 3-inch brass letters spelling "Ehrmanor." The former Ehrmanor is now named Crestview and is owned by the Four Square Church.

Samuel Lancaster suggested Crown Point as a site for an observatory to recognize "the trials and hardships of those who had come into the Oregon country" and from which the Gorge "could be viewed in silent communion with the infinite." In August, 1916, farmers with Fresnos and wagons started excavating the foundation for the Vista House at Crown Point. Construction, impeded somewhat by the severe winds and winter conditions at Thor's Point, took 20 months. The reinforced concrete, Ashlar sandstone-faced, octagonal structure designed by architect Edgar M. Lazarus is a fitting tribute to the pioneers that it memorializes. It features Alaska marble floors, artglass windows, brass handrails and a terra-cotta tile roof. An organization, the "Friends of the Vista House," helped raise funds for a complete renovation of both the interior and exterior of this beautiful, historic building, which project was completed at a cost of more than $4 million. Now part of the Oregon Parks and Recreation Department, its "Friends" management rejoiced in the re-opening of the historic Vista House to the public in June, 2005. On May 5, 2006, at a ceremony held exactly 88 years after the structure was first dedicated as a memorial to Oregon's pioneers, Governor Ted Kulongoski re-dedicated the completely renovated Vista House, with two alterations; wheel chair access and a "lift" to the lower level.

In the early 1920s, George and Nettie Johnson opened an ice cream parlor that soon became Johnson's Vista Café. Situated in an ideal location within an easy stroll of the Vista House, the restaurant profited from the many visitors who stopped there. In the 1930s, the United States Weather Bureau established a weather station in a small back room in the café. The station provided hourly reports to the main Portland weather station until it closed on October 21, 1945. When tour busses unloaded passengers at the restaurant, the weather station employees often had to "pitch in" to help with the dishes or other restaurant chores.

On June 4, 1925, Grace H. Palmer's "tea house," designed by Portland architect Carl Linde, opened its doors to the public. Constructed on the ridge above Crown Point, the *Gresham Outlook* characterized it as another "summer resort." In 1927, Palmer sold the restaurant to William Moessner, a chef trained in Germany. Moessner renamed it the View Point Inn, a fitting name given its stunning view of the Columbia River Gorge and the lights of the Portland metropolitan area. The Inn, with Mr. Moessner in the kitchen and his wife, Clara, as hostess, attracted a clientele of business and political leaders as well as charter-bus patrons. Moessner operated the business from 1917 to 1962. He continued to make the inn his home until his death in 1979. Though listed on the National Register of Historic Places, Multnomah County and the Columbia River Gorge Commission failed, until recently (2005), to recognize the historic and cultural values of the inn to the Gorge. The View Point Inn is the only survivor of ten restaurants built within a five-mile radius after completion of the CRH [see "Notes," p. 263]. Unfortunately, though the Gorge Commission amended its management plan to permit the historic inn to open, Multnomah County's planning department has repeatedly impeded the process. On November 8, 2006, however, a neutral hearings officer ruled favorably on the inn's application to open. Since the newly elected commission chair, Ted Wheeler, has expressed his support for the historic inn's re-opening, perhaps the ordeal its owners have experienced is over.

Ehrmanor (a.k.a. Crestview Manor), Columbia Heights

Edward Ehrman, wholesale grocer, commissioned A.E. Doyle, noted Portland architect, to design and build this beautiful mansion on his estate in the Gorge.

Ehrmanor

Ehrman Mansion (English cottage style) and pool, looking west.

Photos courtesy of the Four Square Church.

90

Julius Meier Estate, Menucha

In 1915, Julius Meier had architect A.E. Doyle design and build this rustic mansion in the "Craftsman Movement" style (use of natural materials) as a summer home on his Gorge estate
.
Photo courtesy of George Perry VI.

Meier's Second Mansion

A new Menucha mansion (1927) replaced the first, which suffered from insect damage to its log pillars. *Photo, the author's collection.*

The Chanticleer Inn, 1912-1930

In 1912, Alba and Madge Kay Morgan built this restaurant before the CRH came through. They christened the location, "Chanticleer Point," perhaps because of its proximity to Rooster Rock on the river below. Hostess (partner?) Margaret Henderson's culinary skills and flair gave the inn a rousing start. On August 27, 1913, the Multnomah County Commission met here and voted to construct a highway through the Gorge. (The automobiles are Pierce-Arrows, probably 1911 or 1912 models.)   *Photo, artist Charles W. Post.*

In The Spirit of the Times

Neighbor Bob Knieriem (Knieriem Road), in a 1911 Winton, visits the Chanticleer Inn, to which hostess Margaret Henderson's celebrated hospitality drew throngs.

Photo courtesy of Bob Dunken.

Crown Point from Chanticleer Point, 1914

Crown Point (under construction) and the Columbia River Gorge from Chanticleer Point.

Photo, artist Charles W. Post.

Monument to Sam Hill, Road Builder

Sam Hill Monument, Columbia River Highway, Portland Women's Forum State Scenic Over-look.

Photo postcard courtesy of Steve Lehl.

The Crowston Place ca 1898

The former Hicks Home, Chanticleer Point, is directly across the highway from the Portland Women's Forum State Park. It is now (2006) owned by Jennifer O'Donnell, who is restoring and renovating the structure.   *Photo courtesy of Laura Hicks.*

The Summit, Jim Ross, 1914

The Summit, where Jim Ross built an ice cream shop for his daughter, Laura Ross. He added the service bay shown in 1915.   *Photo courtesy of Herb Salzman.*

The Gorge from the Summit

View of Rooster Rock and the Columbia River from the Summit (highest point on the CRH). The structure near Rooster Rock (left middle) is Patrick McGowan's salmon cannery.

Photo postcard courtesy of Steve Lehl.

The View Point Inn

In 2005, the Columbia River Gorge Commission amended its Management Plan to allow the View Point Inn to operate in its historic tradition. Despite Multnomah County Planning Department efforts, a neutral hearings officer ruled favorably on the owners' application to open. Consequently, the historic inn may soon be open to the public once again.

Photo, the author.

Retaining Wall Topped by Guard Rocks

This retaining wall topped with Guard Rocks is found between the Summit and Crown Point. (Middle left, Chanticleer Point, with Onion Rock and Tunnel Point [framed] at river level).

1914 photos courtesy of George Perry VI.

Retaining Wall Topped by a Standard-Arch Masonry Guard Rail

This standard arch rail, also found between the summit and Crown Point, remains in place and continues to frame Rooster Rock. Note the unpaved highway surface.

Thor's Point, 1912

Thor's Point (later, Crown Point) before Samuel Lancaster's viaduct circled the Point. Early settlers, aware of the severe winter conditions at the Point, gave it the name, Thor's Point, for the Norse god of thunder and lightning.   *Photo, artist Charles W. Post.*

Constructing the Highway, Thor's Point

Construction of the Columbia River Highway through the Gorge proved to be a challenging, engineering undertaking, particularly at Thor's Point. Samuel C. Lancaster was equal to the task.   *Photo courtesy of George Perry VI.*

Construction Detail, Thor's Point Viaduct, 1914

The CRH under construction around Thor's (Crown) Point in 1914. The highway fill is held by a stone retaining wall; a viaduct with concrete columns supports the walk. Light standards were placed every 20-feet along the protective rail that circled the point.

Oregon Department of Transportation photo courtesy of Robert Hadlow.

Crown Point Viaduct, 1914

The Viaduct around Thor's Point is completed. Note Rooster Rock in the right foreground.

Photo courtesy of George Perry VI.

Construction Detail, Thor's Point, 1914

Workers lay the highway roadbed within the supporting retaining wall and viaduct circling Thor's Point. *Photos, artist Charles W. Post.*

The Completed and Paved Highway at Crown Point, 1916

The Columbia River Highway roadbed was completed and paved beyond Multnomah Falls by late October, 1915. This photograph had to be taken before August, 1916, as construction of the Vista House commenced then.

Margaret Henderson's Crown Point Chalet

The Crown Point Chalet, built in 1915 on the ridge above Crown Point, was patronized by tourists, including the wealthy and famous, until it closed in 1927 after Margaret Henderson was injured in a fall.   *Photo, artist Charles W. Post.*

Interior Dining Area (and Ballroom), Crown Point Chalet

Margaret Henderson's father, H.L. Darling, prominent wood craftsman and cabinet maker, applied his talent in completing the interior appointments of the Chalet.

Photo courtesy of Elizabeth (Morgan)Tanner.

Work Commences on the Vista House

Farmers, using Fresnos and wagons, start excavating for the foundation of the Vista House, August, 1916.   *Photo, artist Charles W. Post.*

Construction Detail, The Vista House, 1917-18

The severe winter of 1917-18 (left) temporarily stopped work on the Vista House, but work resumed in the spring. Construction crews had completed the job in late April, 1918.

Photos, Herb Salzman and George Perry VI. respectively.

Stone Work on the Vista House

Above: Stonemasons apply the Ashler sandstone exterior to the Vista House; Below: The Vista House in the spring of 1918, with the stone facade completed.

Top photo courtesy of Zora Leona McCallum; Bottom photo courtesy of Steve Gillmer.

The Completed Vista House and Viaduct, April, 1918

Stone work detail of the retaining wall that supports the fill on which the Vista House was built. Notice the fact that stonemasons used mortar in the staircase area. (Note the Crown Point Chalet behind the Vista House.)   *Photo, Cross & Dimmitt*

Vista House Superb, April, 1918

The completed, magnificent Vista House, designed by Edgar M. Lazarus, situated on a point above the Columbia River, commands a sweeping view of the beautiful Columbia River Gorge.

Photo courtesy of George Perry VI.

Dedication of the Vista House, May 5, 1918

The dedication ceremony took place during the war years [World War I]. Photo, Cross & Dimmitt.

Stage Tour

Kurt and Augusta Bruune tour the Columbia River Highway in this Columbia Stages touring bus, which took tourists from Portland west to Seaside and east to The Dalles on the new highway. Photo courtesy of Bob Wenzel.

Crown Point's "Crown"

Light standards placed every 20-feet along the outer edge of the viaduct at Crown Point gave Thor's Point a "crown" when lighted. Photo, the artist Charles W. Post.

A Historic Oregon Landmark, The Vista House

The magnificent Vista House, a landmark in the Columbia River Gorge since its completion in 1918, memorializes Oregon's Pioneers. Photo, George Perry VI.

Crown Point

Johnson's Vista Cafe (left), which housed the U.S. Weather Bureau Station, and the Vista House.
Photo postcard courtesy of Steve Lehl.

Lancaster's "King of Roads" Circles Crown Point

This aerial photograph captures the brilliance and genius of Samuel Lancaster, who designed the Columbia River Highway through the Columbia River Gorge. Margaret Henderson's Crown Point Chalet (right foreground), Johnson's Vista Café (right center) and the town of Latourell (upper right) are also visible   *Photo, Brubacker Aerial Survey.*

Johnson's Vista Café and the Vista House

Johnson's Vista Café, Nettie Johnson (right), proprietor. Later, the U.S. Weather Station was located in a room at this end of the restaurant.

Johnson's Vista Café and Service Station, Crown Point

Left, Jack Waldrow's Oregon State Police patrol car in front of Johnson's Vista Café. Officer Waldrow frequently dined at the café. Right, Ned Johnson mans the pumps at the family's Standard station.   *Photos courtesy of George Johnson.*

The East Wind Plays Havoc

The East Wind takes its toll, Crown Point. The truck appears to be an early 1930s model. It has an opening for a hand crank.　　　　　　*Photos courtesy of George Johnson.*

The Vista House

The Vista House often has an ice or snow "facade" in winter months.

Winter Scene at Crown Point

Another winter scene; Vista House and Johnson's Vista Cafe, 1930s. (The first automobile [left] appears to be a mid-1930s Terraplane.)   *Photo courtesy of George Johnson.*

Gorge View West From Crown Point, 1916

Rooster Rock, McGowan's Salmon Cannery, an Oregon/Washington Railroad and Navigation Company train and the Columbia River (west) from Crown Point.   *Photo, artist Charles W. Post.*

East Approach, Crown Point

This automobile has circled Crown Point and is headed for the Figure Eight and Latourell.
Photo, artist Charles W. Post.

Construction Detail Below Crown Point

The CRH below Crown Point, under construction, including stone work.   *Photos, George Perry VI.*

Stone Work Below Crown Point

This retaining wall topped by a standard-arch masonry rail is below Crown Point.

Photo courtesy of George Perry VI.

The Curves of the Figure Eight

Samuel Lancaster, through the use of broad curves, took the highway from Crown Point to Latourell without violating his "5%" grade standard. (The automobile is an early Model-T Ford.)

Photo, artist Charles W. Post.

Latourell Landing ca 1890

In its heyday, Latourell served as a center for commerce and social activities for the hinterland above. The Latourell Band greeted visitors at the landing and played dance music for them at the park pavillion. The "doings" at Latourell attracted people by trail, by train and by steamboat.   *Photo courtesy of John Kerslake.*

Latourell's First Automobile

When the new highway came through Latourell, Knutsen Courter (rear) purchased this 1912 Cadillac (driver, Herb Courter). Unfortunately for Latourell, the new highway provided a means for its residents and others to drive to other towns, which caused Latourell to lose its importance.   *Photo courtesy of Bob Dunken.*

Multnomah County - Latourell and Vicinity

The Highway: As described by Samuel Lancaster, the highway from Crown Point to Latourell was "cut from solid rock for the first mile and hangs on the steep sides of the mountain. A little further on it was necessary to loop back and forth through the beautiful forest...in order to 'develop' distance and come down on the maximum grade of 5 per cent..." to reach Latourell Falls. Lancaster praised the design of the bridge across Falls Creek. "The bridge is both economical and attractive. The type is original, being entirely different from anything yet attempted in this country. This and all other reinforced concrete bridges and viaducts on the Columbia Highway in Multnomah County were designed by K.P. Billner, who is entitled to full praise for his splendid accomplishments." The 312-foot "lace-like" concrete, trussed-arch structure has three 80-foot arches and stands 100 feet above the creek. At Latourell, the "waterfalls section" of the highway begins. In addition to his concern that the highway be built in harmony with its surroundings, Lancaster wrote that he planned the location of the highway in such a way as to make the Gorge's "beauty spots" accessible. He achieved this goal with respect to Gorge waterfalls. In addition, the highway's features, such as its stone retaining walls, standard-arch guard rails, guard rocks, observation points (such as the Eagles Nest) and ancillary projects, all contributed to making "Lancaster's Road" a marvel of the time.

Initially, because of its access to the river and to the railroad, Latourell became a focal point for the settlement of the "mountain" communities to its south. Two wagon roads led to the hinterland above Latourell; the first led to Mountain Grade School and Springfield (Egypt) and the second to the milltown of Brower. Also, settlers used the "wire trail" to reach Latourell from Columbia Heights and Upper Corbett. Joe Latourell founded the town, which became a gateway for settlement and a center for commerce until the Columbia River Highway provided another avenue for the communities of Brower, Egypt, Mountain and Columbia Heights to access markets and obtain supplies. Joseph Latourell (originally, Latourelle), a young man of French ancestry from Keysville, New York, started what became an epic journey at age 20. Born of French-Canadian parents, he was orphaned at an early age. Packing his belongings, including his valued violin, he shipped aboard a whaler bound for the Arctic. After a two-year adventure in the far north, he found his way to San Francisco, where he was shanghaied on a ship headed back to the Arctic for whales and skins. He managed to escape his captors at Fort Vancouver. Fleeing up the north bank of the Columbia River, he found a home with Richard and Betsy Ough. He worked on the Ough farm for several years. Each year, Latourell ferried Ough's stock across the river to the rich grazing land lying below Thor's Heights (Crown Point). Latourell liked the land, and in 1856 (or '57) decided to settle in Oregon. He proposed to Richard and Betsy Ough's daughter, Grace, and filed for a homestead near Rooster Rock. On February 14, 1859, Joseph Latourell and Grace Ough married and moved into a log cabin on the homestead. Later, the log house gave way to a big farm house where they reared their eight children. When a school opened near Chanticleer Point (affiliated with the Troutdale District, according to Lydia [Taylor] Ostrand), the older Latourell children attended there, where she taught. The children then completed their education in Portland at either Central High (where the Meier and Frank department store now stands) or North High (where Good Samaritan hospital is situated).

A small town developed around the Latourell home, which was given the name Latourell to honor its founder. When the telegraph company placed its line along the old Indian trail that connected the two trading points, Celilo and the falls at Oregon City, the company employed Joseph Latourell as an operator and lineman. Soon the community of Latourell became the social center for much of the surrounding countryside. Settlers gathered at Latourell's store and at the saloon to meet their neighbors and to hear the news from the outside world. The Latourells used the log dwelling to house travelers or neighbors who wished to remain overnight. He sponsored dances, for which, Lydia Ostrand recalled, "[Joe Latourell] provided the music, as he was a good fiddler. Grace Latourell provided the midnight supper. Because of the fact that there were no roads and most of the people came to the dance either by way of the trails or by boat, they did not attempt to go home in the dark, so the dance always lasted till daylight." Some accounts suggest that Latourell had a small place (described as a dugout or den) where gambling took place almost without letup.

For many years Latourell boated along the Columbia River in his 90-foot "fore 'n after," *Alice Julia*. Apparently, he was the first man to take a large boat through the Cascade rapids to reach the middle river. Joseph and his eldest son, Henry, sailed the *Alice Julia* in the middle river for many years. Before the OR & N line came, Latourell would meet river boats at Rooster Rock to pick up the mail. When the postal service established a post office at Latourell, Joseph Latourell served as its first postmaster. He established the first mercantile store in Latourell. The younger Latourell children attended Mountain Grade School, which was reached via the old Latourell Road up a steep climb to the ridge above Crown Point. (The same grade from Crown Point to Latourell that challenged Samuel Lancaster's engineering expertise.) The Latourells led the effort to construct a school at Latourell, a large two-room schoolhouse with a second story used for a dance hall. Later generations used the upstairs hall for skating, basketball games and meetings. The abandoned building still stands in Latourell.

In its early days, Latourell grew to be quite a thriving little town with a sizable population. There were several business establishments, including a creamery and cheese factory, a dozen or more two-story buildings and many houses on both sides of Falls Creek. The town had its own brass band for many years. The hospitality of the Latourell home was well known. Joseph was quite an entertainer with his fiddling, jig dancing and singing of French ballads. Grace was known for her good meals and was always ready to nurse the neighborhood's sick when called, day or night. With the first piano in the district and several members of the family being musical, the Latourell home became a gathering place for young folks. Joseph and Grace were called "grandpa" and "grandma" by many young people who knew them well. Often there was a houseful of guests, who, as mentioned earlier, often stayed overnight after a dance.

About 1900 the Latourells moved from the ranch to a big town house in Latourell where they lived out their lives. They witnessed many changes along the Columbia River. The second generation of Latourells shared many of them. Sternwheelers with a shallow draft often brought visitors from Portland to picnic at Latourell (now Guy W. Talbot State Park). Joseph or Henry Latourell would meet the boats at Rooster Rock and pilot them safely through the slough. The town band greeted visitors at the dock. Inhabitants turned out to see the boats dock, sometimes two at a time. The boats would arrive about noon and leave around 4:00 p.m. The passengers picnicked in the park and danced at the dance pavilion built for that purpose. A whistle blast gave a half-hour warning before sailing time.

Before the turn of the century, the Brower and Thompson sawmills at Brower (on Larch Mountain) sent rough lumber by flume to the planing mill alongside the railroad east of Falls Creek for finishing and shipping. Several years later, the Maffet and Joseph sawmill near Pepper Mountain utilized the flume for the same purpose. After the Latourell planing mill closed, the mills at Bridal Veil and Palmer continued to provide employment for some of Latourell's workers. When Palmer Mill and much of the surrounding countryside burned in 1902, two survivors, Annie and Maud Puckett, were brought to Latourell where Grace Latourell nursed them back to health. They had lain in Brower Creek near their home for hours while the fire passed through. The two girls were weak from exposure and nearly blinded by the smoke. They remained with Mrs. Latourell for several weeks until they regained their health.

Upon completion of the highway, commercial development started immediately. The Maffet family owned the land along Falls Creek below the falls (see page 117), where the new highway bridge spanned the creek. In 1914, Margaret Henderson, who had earlier hosted at the Chanticleer Inn, built, in association with Harold Maffet, the Falls Chalet on the hillside above the highway bridge. In January, 1915, after operating only six months, the Falls Chalet burned, a temporary set back for Henderson. However, the loss did not dash her entrepeneurial spirit as she quickly found another location above Crown Point to start anew. After the fire, her "silent" partner, Harold Maffet, built his Falls Villa on the north side of the highway at the east end of the bridge. Maffet's Falls Villa opened in June, 1915, only five months after fire destroyed the Chalet. Maffet remodeled and made extensive additions to the Villa in 1923. In the late '20s, Harold Maffet and George Joseph took a "giant," a gravity-fed water cannon, to blast away the hillside across the highway to give Villa patrons a better view of Latourell Falls. A subsequent owner added a gift shop on the south side of the highway. Another commercial development included a garage and service station built near the west entry to the town of Latourell. The new highway provided Latourell residents with a route to reach other communities more easily. Consequently, when Henry Shoults' grocery store in Latourell burned in November, 1916, he did not rebuild.

Latourell Falls

In 1929, Latourell Falls and the surrounding area were given to the state of Oregon by the Guy W. Talbot family, which gift formed Talbot State Park. After I-80 (now I-84) opened, by-passing Latourell, tourist traffic on the Columbia River Highway declined precipitously. After the State of Oregon purchased the Latourell Falls Villa in 1959, it razed the landmark and added the land to Talbot State Park. Today the former vibrant community of Latourell is quiet; there are no business establishments and few residents compared to its earlier years.

The 249-foot cataract on Falls Creek from the CRH bridge.   *Photo, artist Charles W. Post.*

The George Joseph Farm, Latourell

Attorney George Joseph's Latourell Farm (Joseph, republican candidate for Governor in 1930, died during the campaign).   *Photo courtesy of LouAnn Danforth.*

The Latourell School

The abandoned Latourell School, which officially closed in 1950. The District tuitioned its students to Corbett after 1939.   *Photo courtesy of Geraldean (Crouser) Brooks.*

Maffett Home, Latourell

Harold Maffett inherited this property from his lumberman father, Will Maffett. Maffett transported his mill output from Brower by flume to Latourell, where it could be finished and shipped by rail. In the late 1920s, Harold Maffett used a hydraulic giant to remove the hillside behind the home so that his restaurant customers could view Latourell Falls (center).

Photo courtesy of Herb Salzman.

Talbot Bridge, Columbia River Highway, Latourell

Talbot Bridge, Latourell, 1914 (built by Frank Knieriem and Dave Butler)   *Photo, the author.*

117

Latourell Bridge, 1914

The just-completed, 312-foot Latourell Bridge, designed by K.P. Billner, built by the Pacific Bridge Company.   *Photo courtesy of Steve Lehl.*

Margaret Henderson's Falls Chalet

Margaret Henderson's Falls Chalet, 1914-15 (above Falls Creek and the Latourell Creek bridge).
Photo courtesy of George Perry VI.

Harold Maffett's Original Falls Villa ca 1919

Maffett built the Falls Villa in 1915 after his and Margaret Henderson's Falls Chalet burned in January, 1915 (across the highway - see photo, bottom, previous page).

Photo, artist Charles W. Post.

Latourell Villa

Harold Maffet's Latourell Villa after it was remodeled and enlarged in 1923. While owned and operated by the Bennett family, the State of Oregon purchased and razed the structure, 1959.

Photo postcard courtesy of Steve Lehl.

Highway Bridge Over Latourell Creek

Latourell Creek Bridge, 1914, described by Samuel Lancaster as an "original, being entirely different than anything yet attempted in this country."　　　*Photo courtesy of David Sell.*

Columbia River Highway Near Latourell

The CRH near Latourell. Note the town of Latourell (center) and Crown Point (ridge line, mid-right).　　　*Photo, artist Charles W. Post.*

Waterfalls Section - Shepperd's Dell, Bridal Veil

The Highway: From Latourell to Shepperd's Dell, the highway is fairly level as it traverses the valley floor below Gorge cliffs. Shepperd's Dell is one of the more noted scenic spots on the highway. The arched, reinforced, concrete, 100-foot bridge, designed by K.P. Billner, spans a narrow gorge above Young Creek some 140-feet below. Settler George Shepperd, elated at the prospect of a decent road to his property, donated the right-of-way across his land for the highway. He also donated eleven acres along the creek for a park to honor his wife, Matilda. Samuel Lancaster described the parcel as "unexcelled," and remarked of the donor:

> "Men of wealth and high position have done big things for the Columbia River Highway which will live in history; but George Shepperd, a man of small means, did his part full well."

Just beyond the bridge, Italian stonemasons constructed a retaining wall to hold the fill for the highway, which circumvented Bishop's Cap. The lower portion of the rock was carved away to form a "half-tunnel," which provided clearance needed for vehicular traffic. Another feature of interest is found just past this landmark. Around the corner, stonemasons constructed a "box culvert" to take a small stream under the highway. A retaining wall topped by "guard rocks" supports the highway fill through which the culvert passes. In the next mile, several historic structures are found. First, on the left about one-half mile from Shepperd's Dell, is the Luscher barn, built in the 1870s. Fred Luscher had two teenage sons, Fritz and Ben, both of whom worked with teams to help build the highway. Another farmer, Albert Salzman, who worked with the boys, recalled a conversation he had with the boys' father. According to Salzman, Luscher, relishing the $5.00 per day each boy earned, uttered, in his heavily Swiss-accented voice, "Every two days a twenty." Beyond the Luscher barn on the same side of the highway is a stately structure that opened for business in 1916. Built as a restaurant by Nettie Arnold and Anne Hibler, Forest Hall later came into the possession of Elsa Maxwell, who operated the restaurant as the Maxwell House for many years. The historic structure, owned by Patrick and Patricia Brothers, is now a private residence.

Next, on the right, Henderson Road intersects the highway. A wealthy lumberman attracted to the area was Milton F. Henderson. In 1916, Henderson, a Portland lumberman, purchased property overlooking the Columbia River near Bridal Veil Falls. His estate, Sunset Gables, included a mansion, a carriage house, a tennis court, a lake and landscaped grounds planted to exotic trees, shrubs and flowers. The elegant estate is not visible from the highway. Immediately beyond Henderson Road, another structure of interest is Bridal Veil Lodge, built by Virgil and Lillie Amend. Amend, who worked at the Bridal Veil mill, had purchased land along Bridal Veil Creek from the lumber company. When the highway came through, he started an auto court. Later, he added a lodge (Bridal Veil Lodge), which remains in the family and is now operated as a bed and breakfast by Amend's great-granddaughter, Laurel (Brown) Macdonald. Another early development included a garage and service station near Amend's business complex. In 1948, the Ellesson family purchased the historic Cliff House and associated property. The Ellessons built a restaurant and a motel where Bridal Veil State Park is now situated. The State of Oregon purchased the site for park purposes in 1969.

A concrete-girder bridge directly above Bridal Veil Falls takes traffic across Bridal Veil Creek and into the mill town of Bridal Veil. Loring C. Palmer, mill founder, spent his boyhood years in Wisconsin. At age 17 he enlisted in the Union Army and served until the end of the war in 1865. He entered the lumber business, operating sawmills first in the Dakotas and later in Nebraska. In 1881, Palmer moved west to Vancouver, Washington, where he purchased one mill and managed another, which represented the totality of the lumber business in that city at the time. The center of the lumber business was shifting from the Midwest to the coast during this era, and mills in the Northwest were prospering. Wanting to take advantage of the opportunity, Palmer began an ambitious undertaking.

Lumbermen knew of the vast expanse of fine timber on the slopes of Larch Mountain, but it was considered inaccessible and hence of little interest. Palmer visualized an operation that included a mill located on the mountain together with a flume to carry the mill output to a site close to the railroad along the Columbia River. The rough-cut lumber would be further processed there to make a finished product and shipped to market by rail. Palmer sold his mill in Vancouver and, in 1887, organized the Bridal Veil Lumbering Company.

Bridal Veil Falls gave the company's mill town its name. Supposedly, a lady passenger on the sternwheeler *Bailey Gatzert* looked toward the Oregon shore, noticed the falls tumbling over a Gorge crag and remarked, "That looks just like a bride's veil." When the settlement gained a post office, the official name became Bridal Veil. The town grew as Bridal Veil Lumbering Company prospered. Only two primitive wagon roads served the town; a branch road off the old Latourell Road and the exceedlingly steep road to Palmer, Brower and beyond. Of course, the principal means of transportation was the O R & N line, which had a station at Bridal Veil. Bridal Veil had many single-family company homes as well as three larger structures: a "hotel" for single workers, a store and the Cliff House, the home of one of the firm's partners. The second story of the store provided space for the company's administrative offices.

Bridal Veil Falls

Bridal Veil falls, which can be reached by trail from the Oregon state parks parking lot across from Bridal Veil Lodge.

In 1915, Clarence Jacobson, a well-to-do Portland clothier and his heiress wife, Dorothy, purchased fifteen acres along Coopey Creek near Bridal Veil. The Jacobsons hired Morris H. Whitehouse to design a mansion in the "Italian villa" style. Italian stonemasons, recruited from among the highway workers, were engaged to construct fish ponds, walks, steps, bridges and other stone work on the grounds. A carriage house near the gated entry provided living quarters for the Jacobson's chauffeur and garage space for the couple's automobiles. The plans included a swimming pool, a powerhouse utilizing Coopey Creek to generate electricity and formal gardens, among other amenities. The mansion contained several guest rooms, a full basement and an open, vaulted living room. The former Jacobson mansion is now owned by the Franciscan Sisters of the Eucharist, who are engaged in restoring the building. In 1929, Ray Holtgrieve purchased a restaurant and auto court, formerly part of the Jacobson estate, which had been purchased by William and Louise Lawrence. When prohibition ended, Holtgrieve added a bar. Eventually, he added cabins, obtained drift (fishing) rights on the Columbia River, and built up quite a thriving business complex. Holtgrieve died in 1962 and his descendants sold the various enterprises in 1969. All are now (2006) closed.

From Bridal Veil, the highway descends gradually to the valley floor and parallels the railroad line to Mist Falls, which Lancaster characterized as "a clear wisp of water which falls over the high cliffs in a series of cascades from an elevation of 1500 feet. It is broken and torn and in its last wild leap is lost in mist and spray, for every wind that blows drives it about, and sometimes carries it straight up, before it settles on the trees and vegetation below, to be gathered again into a water brook and continue its way to the sea."

Mist Falls and Mist Lodge

Mist Falls, which Lewis and Clark described as follows: "...while other small streams precipitate themselves from a still greater elevation and evaporating in a mist again collect and form a second cascade before they reach the bottom of the rocks" Mist Lodge opened in 1916; burned in 1929.
Photo postcard courtesy of Steve Lehl.

123

Shepperd's Dell

Shepperd's Dell Bridge, a 150-foot arch span designed by K.P. Billner, 1914.

Bridge Approach, Shepperd's Dell

This worker has just removed the cap form from this standard arch masonry rail at Shepperd's Dell, 1914.   *Photos courtesy of George Perry VI.*

Shepperd's Dell, 1915

Shepperd's Dell Bridge, shortly after completion of this section of the highway.
Photo, artist Charles W. Post.

Shepperd's Dell Bridge and Bishop's Cap

Shepperd's Dell Bridge, the trailhead and Bishop's Cap.   *Photo postcard, Steve Lehl.*

The Spectacular Views at Shepperd's Dell

Above: The stone rail lining the path to Young Creek, 1914 . Below, left: Young Creek cascades over palisades of the Gorge. Below, right: The falls at Shepperd's Dell, framed by the bridge's arches.   Photos, artist Charles W. Post.

The 'half-tunnel' at Bishop's Cap with retaining wall, guard rocks and standard arch masonry rail (1914).   *Photo courtesy of George Perry VI.*

Retaining Wall and Box Culvert Near Bishop's Cap, 1914

This retaining wall and box culvert, built to take a small stream under the highway, is a prime example of the engineering techniques that Samuel Lancaster used to lessen the impact on the natural area by designing a man-made structure of beauty to perform the needed function.

Photos courtesy of George Perry VI.

Forest Hall, 1916

The (former) Forest Hall Restaurant (aka Maxwell House), near Bridal Veil.

Photo postcard courtesy of Steve Lehl.

Sunset Gables, Bridal Veil, 1916

Lumberman Milton F. Henderson's Sunset Gables, Bridal Veil, Oregon.

Photo courtesy of Laurel Cookman.

The Bridal Veil Lodge, 1926

The historic Lodge is now operated as a bed and breakfast by Laurel (Brown) Macdonald, great-granddaughter of the founder.

Cliff House, Bridal Veil

The Cliff House, Bridal Veil.   *Photo postcards courtesy of Steve Lehl.*

The Bridal Veil Mill and Company Town

The Bridal Veil Lumbering Company complex, Bridal Veil, Oregon, est. 1887.

Photo courtesy of the Crown Point Country Historical Society.

Bridal Veil Lumbering Company Flume, 1914

Bridal Veil Lumbering Company flume. From l, Marge Mershon (on stairs), unknown, Fred Smith (on rock), Albert Salzman (partially obscured), Clara Lasley and Laura Wilson. The other individuals on the flume are not identified.   *Photo, the author.*

131

Bridal Veil Lumbering Company Hotel

The Bridal Veil Hotel, built by the Company to house unmarried mill workers.

Photo courtesy of Vito Mosso.

The Jacobson Mansion, Bridal Veil, 1916

Jacobson Mansion, Bridal Veil (now owned by the Franciscan Sisters of the Eucharist),

Photos, artist Charles W. Post.

Waterfalls Section - Wahkeena To Bonneville

From Bridal Veil, the highway descends gradually to the valley floor and parallels the railroad line to Mist Falls, which Lancaster characterized as "a clear wisp of water which falls over the high cliffs in a series of cascades from an elevation of 1500 feet. It is broken and torn and in its last wild leap is lost in mist and spray, for every wind that blows drives it about, and sometimes carries it straight up, before it settles on the trees and vegetation below, to be gathered again into a water brook and continue its way to the sea." Wahkeena Falls (aka Gordon Falls) is the next point of interest. Wahkeena, a series of cascades descending from the heights, is a gorgeous waterfall quite different from the precipitous falls found close by. A rather challenging trail permits the visitor to access this beautiful waterfall. Beyond Wahkeena Falls, the highway crosses a reinforced concrete viaduct, necessitated by the steep talus slopes along which the rail line passed. As Lancaster noted, undercutting the slope would have caused a "disaster, for the whole mountain above for hundreds of feet would then slide down." The 400-foot viaduct solved this problem. After travelers cross the viaduct, the parking area at Multnomah Falls comes into view.

On June 7, 1916, a ceremony held at Multnomah Falls (and other locations) celebrated the completion of the Multnomah County segment of the grand highway. Simon Benson purchased approximately 400 acres in the vicinity of Multnomah Falls that he donated to the City of Portland. His influence and largess are apparent throughout the Gorge: his donations paid for ancillary projects such as the stonework along area trails and the bridge over the chasm above the lower falls, which made possible a trail to reach the top of the falls and beyond for pedestrian travel. Samuel Lancaster took Benson to a point above the lower falls and suggested a bridge at the site would be useful. Benson asked the cost, which Lancaster quickly determined. Benson wrote a check for the amount on the spot and said, "Build it." In 1917, under city oversight, the Hazelwood Creamery Company, J. Harry Joyce, President, opened a "refreshment house" at Multnomah Falls. This business served the tourist trade until replaced, in 1925, by the Multnomah Falls Lodge, designed by A.E. Doyle. The area remained under city ownership until the late 1930s, when Portland transferred ownership to the U.S. Forest Service and the Oregon State Parks Division. Benson State Park honors its benefactor, Simon Benson.

Multnomah Falls, a premier Oregon tourist attraction, drew visitors long before the completion of the Columbia River Highway. Noted by explorers Lewis and Clark on their journey of exploration in 1805-06, the Gorge waterfalls became a destination for steamboat passengers in the early settlement years and for excursion train passengers after 1883. Steamboats made regular stops at the landing east of the falls and the OR & N established a station with a loading platform at Multnomah Falls to accomodate the crowds that its excursion trains brought to the area. Samuel C. Lancaster wrote that he had planned the location of the highway in such a way as to make the Gorge's "beauty spots" accessible by road, which is certainly the case with Multnomah Falls. Nearby cataracts include Mist Falls, Wahkeena Falls, the lower falls on Oneonta Creek and Horsetail Falls. In addition to his work planning the highway, Samuel Lancaster initiated the development of a trail system so that visitors could explore the backcountry above the highway. He helped organize what became the Trails Club and served as its first president. These trails lead the visitor to higher falls, including a series of falls on Multnomah Creek, Wahkeena Falls, Triple Falls on Oneonta Creek and Ponytail Falls above Horsetail Falls, where visitors may walk behind a Gorge waterfall.

Additions were made to the lodge in subsequent years. The present gift shop was added in 1927. Other additions were made in 1950, 1960 and 1994. The latter change added a large complex to the east end of the lodge behind the gift shop. In the 1930s, Civilian Conservation Corps (CCC) recruits built stone campstoves and added other amenities at Benson State Park. CCC members also made other improvements in the area, such as improving and extending the trail system. Today, Multnomah Falls is Oregon's leading natural tourist attraction, hosting more than two million visitors annually.

Another facility, Mist Lodge (aka Multnomah Lodge) pre-dated Multnomah Falls Lodge. Built nearly directly below Mist Falls, the structure suffered severe damage from heavy snow-fall during the winter of 1920-21. The accumulation of snow caused the lodge roof to collapse. That winter, huge snowdrifts blocked the CRH for several weeks and deep, glacier-like drifts near Oneonta were not entirely cleared until spring. After being restored and reopened, Mist Lodge operated until it burned in 1929. Because of the onset of the Depression, it was not rebuilt. Another restaurant operated in the area for a relatively short time. Mrs. W.J. Gebott owned and managed the Jack-O-Lantern, located near Horsetail Falls.

Early settlers and an explorer gave their names to the small communities between Multnomah Falls and Bonneville. Ira Dodson, active in the fishing industry, which included his cannery below St. Peter's Dome, is memorialized by the community of Dodson. The Dodson cannery became associated with the Columbia River Packers' Association. Frank Warren built a cannery, Warren Packing Company, near the mouth of McCord Creek. He also owned several fishwheels that operated in the vicinity. Frank Warren died when the new White Star Line steamship, *Titanic*, sank on April 15, 1912, after striking an iceberg in the North Atlantic. His son, Frank Warren II, was instrumental in the formation of the Portland Port Commission and his grandson, Frank Warren III, presided over Portland General Electric Company for many years. Of course, Warren's namesake is Warrendale. Thomas Moffett home-steaded a narrow bench of land along Moffett Creek, giving his name to the creek and the bridge that spanned it. Samuel Lancaster characterized the Moffett Creek Bridge as the "largest flat arch bridge in America [completed in 1915] and the largest three-hinged arch in the world." Other settlers in the area included Sam Gorman, whose apple orchard planted on the hillside below St. Peter's Dome provided riverboat passengers with a stunning display when his frui t trees bloomed in the spring. William Sams took up a homestead about a mile east of Warrendale and raised a large family.

Wahkeena Falls

Trail, Wahkeena Falls. Retaining wall, stone bridge and rail built by immigrant Italian stonemasons, 1914.   *Photo, artist Charles W. Post.*

Mist Lodge, 1916

Mist Lodge (aka Multnomah Lodge), near Wahkeena Falls (1916-1929).
Photo courtesy of Steve Lehl.

Wahkeena Falls

Left, Wahkeena's Necktie Falls. Right, Wahkeena Falls, Columbia River Highway in the fore-
ground.   *Left: Photo postcard courtesy of Steve Lehl; Right: Photo, artist Charles W. Post.*

Wahkeena Wayside

The pull-off at Wahkeena Falls provided tourists with a place to buy refreshments and a parking spot to permit a walk on the trail along the creek and to Multnomah Falls.

Photo courtesy of David Sell.

Rotary 'Wheel,' Wahkeena Falls

The Rotary Wheel fountain at Wahkeena Falls honored Frank Riggs and the Portland Rotary Club's support for the Columbia River Highway.   *Photo postcard courtesy of Steve Lehl.*

Multnomah Falls

Left: Multnomah Falls, ca 1912. Right: The falls after Samuel Lancaster built the Benson Bridge, ca 1915.   Left photo, the author's collection; right photo, artist Charles W. Post.

Dedication of the Columbia River Highway at Multnomah Falls

Dedication ceremony, Columbia River Highway, Multnomah Falls, June 7, 1916.

Photo courtesy of George Perry VI.

137

Multnomah Falls

The Multnomah Falls Station and an OW R & N. excursion train at Multnomah Falls.
Photo postcards, the author's collection.

Multnomah Falls Parking Area ca 1920

CRH Bridge over Multnomah Creek, built in 1914.   *Photo postcard courtesy of CarolRoyse.*

Hazelwood Dairy's Ice Cream Shop at Multnomah Falls

Multnomah Falls Hazelwood (temporary) gift shop and refreshment house, 1917 to 1925.
Photo postcard courtesy of Steve Lehl.

Multnomah Falls Lodge ca 1925

The Multnomah Falls Lodge, designed by A.E. Doyle, supplanted the Hazelwood Dairy's ice cream "refreshment house" and gift shop.   *Photo postcard courtesy of Steve Lehl.*

139

Multnomah Falls Landing

Steamboat at the Multnomah Falls Landing and the new highway, just east of Multnomah Falls, 1915, before the highway was paved.   *Photos, artist Charles W. Post.*

Oneonta Creek and Oneonta Falls

Oneonta Gorge, 1914. The falls (right) can be reached (at times) by hiking up the creek.

Construction Detail, Oneonta Bluff Tunnel

Road crews construct the Oneonta Bluff tunnel, 1915. The Oregon Highway Commission filled the tunnel with rubble in 1948. Photos Oregon Department of Transportation.

Oneonta Bluff   Horsetail Falls

Oneonta Tunnel. OW R & N. line, the CRH Bridge at Horsetail Falls and the falls. Note Pony Tail Falls above Horsetail. Photos courtesy of George Perry VI and artist Charles W. Post, respectively.

Snowdrifts Near Oneonta, March, 1921

Snowdrifts, CRH near Oneonta, cleared by farmers using shovels, mid-March, 1921.

Photo courtesy of Steve Lehl.

Federal/State Highway Restoration Project, Oneonta Tunnel

ODOT, in a cooperative effort involving the Federal Government, has planned several projects to restore parts of the Columbia River Highway to its original configuration. This project is the re-opening of the Oneonta Tunnel, originally built in 1915; abandoned in 1946. The men (upper right) are Grant McOmie, KATU television, and Robert Hadlow, ODOT.

Photos courtesy of David Sell.

Highway Restoration Project - Guard Rocks

Construction crews work to restore the highway, as near as possible, to its original state. Top left: Unidentified stonemasons rebuild a retaining wall topped by "guard rocks" near Wahkeena Falls. Upper right and middle, near Oneonta: All layers of pavement were removed to reach the first, the "Warrennite" paving material applied in 1915-1916. Retaining walls topped by guard rocks, damaged by nine decades use, were renovated/replaced as needed. Bottom: The completely renovated highway, ready for travel. *Photos courtesy of David Sell.*

Columbia River Highway East of Multnomah Falls, 1914

The new and unpaved Columbia River Highway.   *Photo, artist Charles W. Post.*

The CRH Near Oneonta

The macadamized highway between Multnomah Falls and Oneonta before the Warren Company applied Warrenite in 1916.   *Photo courtesy of David Sell.*

Fish Canneries, Dodson - Warrendale

Above: A view of Ira Dodson's salmon cannery at Dodson from Butler's Eddy on the Washington shore. The barn, center right, is where Joseph Bucher established a dairy in the 1930s. Below: Frank H. Warren's cannery, located at Warrendale, from the Washington shore. Warren lost his life when the White Star Line Titanic struck an iceberg in the Atlantic on April 15, 1912 Photos courtesy of Carol (Bucher) Royse.

Construction of the McCord Creek Bridge, 1915

Construction of the McCord Creek Bridge in 1915. The top photographs were taken in May, the middle photographs in July and the bottom photograph upon the completion of the bridge.

Four upper photos courtesy of the Oregon Department of Transportation; lower photograph courtesy of Steve Lehl.

The Completed McCord Creek Bridge

The 365-foot bridge at McCord Creek was one of the longer spans on the original Columbia River Highway. The I-84 bridge spans McCord Creek in this area, but the beautiful original span has been replaced.   *Photo courtesy of David Sell.*

Construction of the Moffett Creek Bridge, 1915

Construction of the Moffett Creek Bridge started in the spring, 1915. This photograph was taken in April.   *Photo courtesy of the Oregon Department of Transportation.*

Construction of the Moffett Creek Bridge Proceeds, 1915

Construction Proceeds on the Moffett Creek Bridge, 1915. The top (left) photograph in April; the top (right) photograph in May; the middle (left) photograph in July; and the middle (right) photograph in August. The lower photo shows the completed span.

"God's Art Gallery"

In 1915, Samuel C. Lancaster wrote:

"…[God] fashioned the Gorge of the Columbia, fixed the course of the broad river, and caused the crystal streams both small and great to leap down from the crags and sing their never ending songs of joy.

Then He planted a garden, then came and built a beautiful city close by this wonderland. To some He gave great wealth – to every man his talent – and when the time had come for men to break down the mountain barriers, construct a great highway of commerce, and utilize the beautiful, which is 'as useful as the useful,' He set them to the task and gave each his place.

I am thankful to God for His goodness in permitting me to have a part in building this broad thoroughfare as a frame to the beautiful picture which He created."

Of the highway, he wrote:

"…The broad thoroughfare is cut out of solid rock, where the steep sides of the mountain rise abruptly, the road is hung around the face of the cliffs like a ribbon, and is six hundred feet above the valley; all danger points are protected by stone and concrete walls, and the God given beauty of this kingly river may be enjoyed by men and women to the full without fear."

"[The Columbia River Highway] makes it possible for the dwellers in the great metropolis to reach in less than two hours **God's art galleries**." Lancaster spoke of the "great variety of wild beauty"…the "beauty spots" of the Columbia River valley.

A few of Lancaster's "beauty spots" are found on the following pages.

The Figure Eight

The scenic beauty opened to all by the construction of the CRH.   *Photo courtesy of Steve Lehl.*

150

Scenic Attractions, "Lower" Columbia River Highway

Above: Whidby Loops,which took motorists from Clatsop Crest to Wauna. Bottom: Beaver Falls, on the historic highway near Clatskanie.

Top photo courtesy of the Oregon Department of Transportation. Bottom: Photo, the author.

Near Prescott Point

From Prescott Point, the historic highway provided access to Little Jack Falls as it descended into Goble.   *Photo postcard, the author.*

Little Jack Falls ca 2006

The falls can be reached via Little Jack Falls Road off Highway 30 near Prescott. The old highway has been cleared a short distance from the access road (see p. 37).   *Photo, the author.*

152

The Gorge From Chanticleer Point

Crown Point and the Columbia River Gorge from Chanticleer Point (Portland Women's Forum State Scenic Viewpoint). *Photo postcard, the author.*

Tunnel Point From Crown Point

A view of Tunnel Point, Reed Island and the Columbia River looking west from Crown Point.
From a painting by artist Charles W. Post.

The Gorge From Crown Point

A view of the Columbia River Gorge from the Vista House, looking east. The photograph shows the light standards placed every 20 feet along the outer viaduct, which gave Thor's Point a "crown." Photo postcard, the author.

Latourell Falls

Shepperd's Dell Bridge - Bishop's Cap

Top: The arched, reinforced concrete Shepperd's Dell Bridge, designed by K.P. Billner. Bottom: The "half tunnel" at Bishop's Cap, Shepperd's Dell.

Photos courtesy of the Oregon Department of Transportation.

Wahkeena Falls

Left: Photo courtesy of the ODOT.   Right: June 7, 1916, CRH dedication tour group stops at Wahkeena.

Multnomah Falls

Oneonta Bluff

Horsetail Falls

Highway Construction Near Bonneville

Top left: From a painting of Oneonta Bluff, artist unknown, owned by the Portland Women's Forum.

    Top right and bottom: Archival photographs courtesy of the Oregon Department of Transportation.

The Highway At Wauna Point

The highway circling Wauna Point provided an overlook to view the Columbia River and Bradford Island, a most scenic area where, Samuel Lancaster noted, the highway passes through the Cascade Divide. Two viaducts, Tooth Rock (above) and Eagle Creek (below), took the highway around the point.   The top photo (courtesy of the Oregon Department of Transportation) shows the Tooth Rock viaduct; The lower photo, the Eagle Creek viaduct (photo postcard, the author).

Inspiration Point, Historic Columbia River Highway State Trail

Rowena Loops, Wasco County

Archival photographs courtesy of the Oregon Department of Transportation.

Oregon's Proposed Highway System, Fourth Biennial

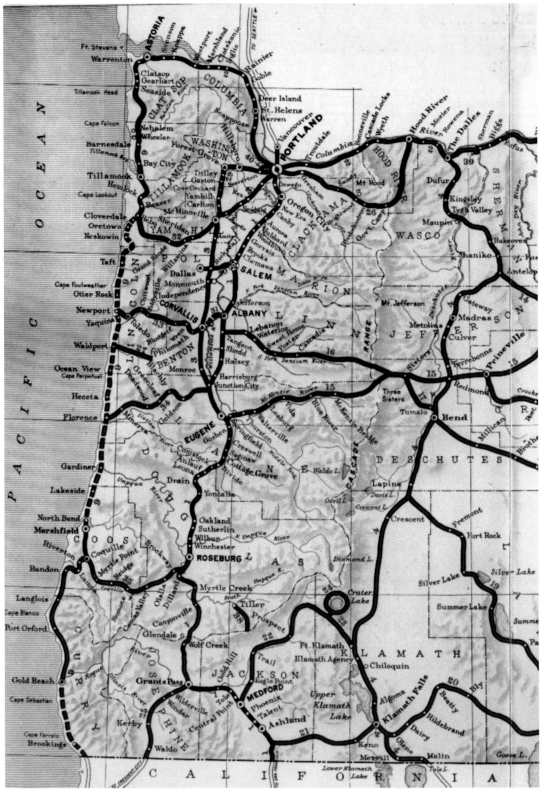

By 1920, under the leadership of Simon Benson, The Oregon Highway Commission (OHC) had made ambitious plans for highway construction in the State of Oregon. The department had forty highway projects underway, with a projected distance of 4,458 miles.

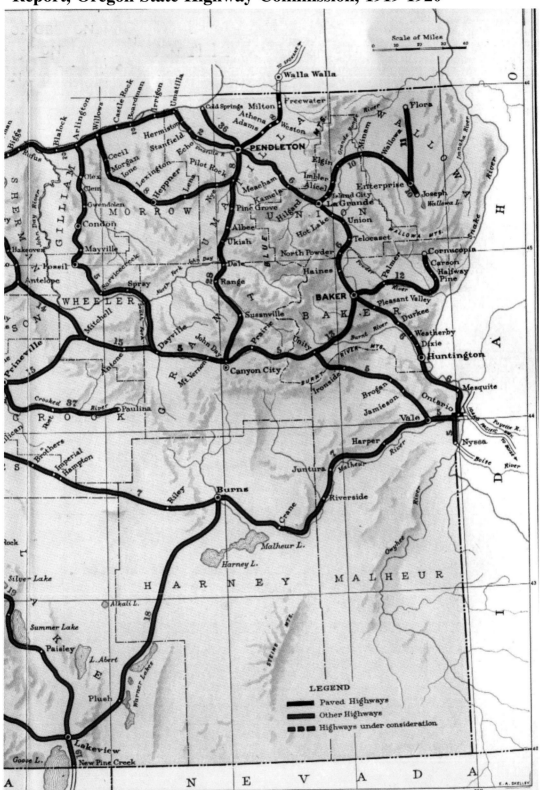

The Columbia River Highway, at 340 miles, was the furthest along. In 1920, Oregon ranked fourth in the nation in expenditures for roads, surpassed only by New York, Pennsylvania and Illinois. *Photo, OHC Fourth Biennial Report, courtesy of Dennis Wiancko.*

Vintage Vehicles

1909 Buick

1909 Brush Run-about

1911 Ford Model T

1924 Ford Model T

Gravity-Feed Gas Pump

1927 Federal

1909 Maxwell

1910 Cadilac: Owners, Bob and Betty Dunken.

*1919 American LaFrance
Fire Engine*

*1926 Peerless "Boat Tail" Roadster
Photos courtesy of Bob Dunken.*

Multnomah County - Bonneville and Eagle Creek

The terrain from Multnomah Falls eastward to Cascade Locks required the ingenuity of an engineer of Samuel Lancaster's calibre. The fact that Gorge cliffs closed on the river in many locations, and the O W R & N. rail line tended to hug the cliffs in those areas, presented Lancaster with many challenges. In addition, many streams carried water from the Gorge's noted waterfalls, which created other obstacles. For example, bridging McCord Creek below Elowah Falls required a 356-foot span, designed by engineer Karl P. Bilner. Lewis W. Metzger designed the longest three-hinged, reinforced concrete arch span of its day to bridge Moffett Creek; a 170-foot span with a rise of only 17 feet. Ralph Modjeski, noted engineer brought to Portland to design the Broadway Bridge, served as a consultant for the project. A short span across Tanner Creek took the highway into Bonneville.

From Bonneville to Cascade Locks, the highway had to cross the divide of the Cascade Mountain Range. Since the O W R & N line had pre-empted the limited space below the cliffs of Wauna Point, Lancaster had to take the highway across the divide along the face of the cliffs. He accomplished this by designing two viaducts, one that took the highway to the cut at Tooth Rock and the second, the Eagle Creek viaduct, that carried the roadbed from the divide at Tooth Rock around Wauna Point to the descent into Eagle Creek. Of course this stretch required the usual Lancaster touch of gentle curves to reach the desired level to cross Eagle Creek. The 144-foot, center-arch span across Eagle Creek is the only bridge on the Columbia River Highway with a native stone facing and stone guard rails. In 1915, the immediate area became part of the Oregon National Forest. The first U.S. Forest Service campground in the nation was established on the eastern bank of Eagle Creek south of the bridge.

The explorer, Captain Benjamin D. Bonneville, gave his name to that locale. Personnel at the Bonneville Fish Hatchery, established by the State of Oregon in 1909, continue to work with fish stocks, including salmon, steelhead, sturgeon, trout and other species. The hatchery maintains observation pools stocked with different fish, rearing ponds and an observation deck for viewing activities during fish runs.

The portage railway that transported goods around the lower and upper Cascade rapids started near Bonneville. A river boat in the lower river would unload its cargo bound for upriver communities at Bonneville, then take on cargo bound for Portland or other lower river destinations. The portage railway transported goods both directions, bypassing the rapids. Its upper station served river boats in the middle river above the upper Cascade Rapids (see p. 211).

In 1933, the federal government commenced the construction of Bonneville Dam, a large power, flood control and waterway project. The dam, built at a cost of $84,000,000, was dedicated by President Franklin D. Roosevelt in 1937. Its fish ladders enable spawning salmon and other species to pass over the dam. Its reservoir covered the lower and upper Cascade rapids and its ship lock allowed ocean going vessels to proceed up the Columbia River as far as The Dalles. Because of the project, some segments of the original CRH had to be relocated. During the construction of the dam, the state highway department completed (in 1936) the Tooth Rock Tunnel, which took the highway under an interesting, if difficult, section of the old highway. The closed portion was recently reopened as part of the Historic Columbia River Highway State Trail.

163

Samuel Lancaster built a private 72-acre campground at Bonneville that overlooked Bradford Island and the lower Cascade rapids. He constructed a log dining hall and tent "cabins" at camping areas. Lancaster used facilities he had observed in Switzerland as a model for his development. The log structure burned in the late 1920s and was not replaced. In 1928, Sam Hill built a 22-room home on a 35-acre estate at Bonneville for his "friend," Mona Bell. Because the property was required for the construction of Bonneville Dam, the government purchased the estate in 1934. Hill was awarded $72,500 plus interest, nearly three times the government's first offer. In the 1930s, Civilian Conservation Corps crews made many improvements to the Eagle Creek campground, adding several structures, including a new comfort station, community kitchen, trail registry booth and an enclosed dining hall with restrooms in the overlook area. The men also built picnic tables, stone camp stoves, water fountains and stone retaining walls for an enlarged picnic area. The trail system was improved and extended.

O W R & N. Train Approaches Bonneville

An Oregon/Washington Railroad & Navigation train passes the Moffett Creek Bridge as it approaches Bonneville Station.   *Photo courtesy of George Perry VI.*

Bonneville Station on the O W R & N.

Bonneville Station, a destination for customers of the O W R & N, who wished to see the fish hatchery. Photo postcard courtesy of Steve Lehl

Union Pacific Station, Bonneville, 1937

Heavy snow the winter of 1936-37 stranded some trains in the Gorge.

Bonneville Fish Hatchery, Tanner Creek

The Bonneville Fish hatchery has been augmenting and supplementing runs of salmon and other species since 1909.   *Photo postcard courtesy of Steve Lehl.*

The Bonneville Fish Hatchery, Bonneville, Oregon

Bonneville Fish Hatchery, 1915. From left, Marge Mershon, Laura Wilson (the author's mother), George Mershon (the author's father), Clara Lasley and an unidentified individual.

      Photo, the author.

Construction of the Tanner Creek Bridge, 1915

Oregon Highway Commission photographs, taken on May 15, 1915 and July 5, 1915, respectively.

Photos courtesy of the Oregon Department of Transportation.

Wauna Point at Bonneville presented one of the more challenging obstacles to face Samuel Lancaster and construction crews. Two viaducts took the highway around the point from which it descended to the bridge across Eagle Creek.   *Photos courtesy of ODOT.*

Construction of the Eagle Creek Viaduct, 1915

The Eagle Creek viaduct completed the circuit around Wauna Point and Tooth Rock. Wauna Point presented one of the more difficult engineering challenges encountered during the construction of the highway. Photos courtesy of the Oregon Department of Transportation (ODOT).

Stonemasons At Work

Rocks, conveyed to the job site as shown in this photograph, had to be placed by hand in the structure. Guard rocks often weighed more than a ton.   Photo courtesy of an anonymous source.

Columbia River Highway, Tooth Rock

The completed viaducts at Toothrock, shown under construction on the previous page.
Left, photo postcard, Steve Lehl; right, photo courtesy of David Sell.

Eagle's Nest, Eagle Creek Viaduct, Wauna Point

Touring the CRH near Bonneville, 1919. This section was abandoned when the tunnel (page 175) was opened in 1936. *Photo courtesy of Herb Salzman.*

Cascades Section, CRH

The CRH (and Eagle Creek viaduct, shown) traversed the promotory at Wauna Point, one of the more spectacular sections of the marvelous highway. *Photo courtesy of George Perry VI.*

Construction of Bonneville Dam, 1933-1938

Top: Construction detail, the powerhouse, looking toward Bradford Island. Middle and bottom: Construction detail, the spillway, 1936 and 1937.

Top photo courtesy of Steve Lehl. Middle and bottom photos courtesy of George Perry VI.

Detail, Bonneville Dam

Left, the fish ladder, designed to allow spawming fish to ascend to the pool behind the dam.
Right, the ship lock, designed to permit the passage of ships and barges past the dam.

Photos courtesy of Rosetta Henkle.

Dedication of Bonneville Dam

Left, President Franklin D. Roosevelt, who dedicated the Bonneville Dam on September 28,
1937. The individual to President Roosevelt's immediate left is not identified; next is Governor
Julius Meier, Oregon. The 4th individual is also not identified.

Photo courtesy of Frieda O'Neil.

Bonneville, Winter, 1936-37

Bonneville Safeway store, Roosevelt Café and the Bonneville Hotel, 1937.

Photo courtesy of Terry Anderson.

Tyrrell Tavern, Bonneville

Tyrrell Tavern, Columbia River Highway, Bonneville.

Photo postcard, Steve Lehl.

Construction of Bonneville Dam Causes Relocation of the CRH

The construction of Bonneville Dam required the re-alignment of a section of the CRH, which eliminated the toothrock segment (left, and preceding pages) with a new highway, a new bridge across Eagle Creek and the toothrock tunnel (below).

Top left photo courtesy of Steve Lehl; right and lower photos courtesy of David Sell.

Construction of the Eagle Creek Bridge, 1915

Both photographs were taken in July, 1915. The 144-foot concrete arch-span took the highway across Eagle Creek, a most scenic area on the highway. *Photos courtesy of ODOT.*

Observation Point, Eagle Creek Bridge ca 1920

The stone-clad Eagle Creek Bridge with its arch masonry rail and observation deck was unique on the Columbia River Highway.   *Photo postcard, the author.*

Eagle Creek

The 144-foot bridge with its 60-foot concrete arch span is the only CRH bridge with a facing of native stone.   *Photo courtesy of Steve Lehl.*

East Approach, Eagle Creek Bridge

This beautiful bridge took the new Columbia River Highway across Eagle Creek.

Photos courtesy of Steve Lehl.

The Approach to Cascade Locks

The CRH between Eagle Creek and Cascade Locks.

Hood River County - The Cascade Rapids and Vicinity

After the United States took over Fort Vancouver in 1846, the need to supply military expeditions fighting Indians east of the Cascades created logistical problems. In 1849 and 1850, bateaux manned by natives transported supplies to these troops. The need for a road was apparent. However, the Cascade Mountains, with sheer cliffs lining the Columbia River for miles, presented a formidable obstacle to road engineers. In the mid-1850s, construction of a military road to supply these garrisons commenced. In 1872, the Oregon Legislature appropriated $50,000 for a wagon road from the Sandy River to The Dalles, followed by an additional appropriation of $50,000 in 1876. According to Samuel C. Lancaster, the wagon road was "crooked and narrow, and the grades were steep...only traces of it could be found in 1913." In 1913, Hood River County requested that the Oregon State Highway Commission make a survey for a highway some 22 miles across the northern portion of the County.

The survey laid out the course of the projected highway starting just west of Cascade Locks. As planned, the highway would follow the old military road from the Multnomah-Hood River County line to a point about four miles east. The road would then skirt the base of Shell Rock Mountain, which had proved to be a nearly impassable barrier to earlier attempts to construct a road. The projected road, from Wyeth to Viento, would follow the base of the cliffs. From Viento, the road would generally follow the old wagon road to Mitchell Point. At Mitchell Point, the highway would depart from the old wagon road to pass along the face of a cliff to Mitchell Point, through which a magnificent tunnel would be bored to make a passage for the road. From Mitchell Point, the new highway would follow the wagon road for about one-half mile, then veer south to avoid rail crossings and climb Ruthton Hill. From Ruthton Hill, the planned highway would follow the old wagon road into Hood River.

In 1914, voters of Hood River County approved a $75,000 bond issue to finance construction of certain sections of the highway. When the issue went unsubscribed, Simon Benson bought the entire issue at par so that construction could begin. On July 6, 1915, the Columbia River Highway was officially opened from Portland to Hood River. In 1917, grading improved the highway between Cascade Locks and Hood River. Further improvement projects were completed in 1918, including hard surfacing of the highway from Cascade Locks to Hood River.

The Mitchell Point Tunnel deserves special mention. Samuel C. Lancaster, consulting engineer whose engineering genius brought him immense acclaim once the highway was completed, wrote: "...The tunnel in the face of the cliff at Mitchell Point, with the concrete viaduct approaches, may well be considered among the most wonderful pieces of highway construction in the civilized world. It is fully equal to the famous Axenstrasse of Switzerland and one of the great features of the highway." No longer! In 1966, Oregon Highway Commission Chairman Glenn Jackson and Governor Mark Hatfield, demonstrating both a total lack of historic perspective and a lack of an appreciation for the accomplishments of others, permitted the dynamiting of the Mitchell Point Tunnel. Blowing up the tunnel permitted the Highway Department to widen the freeway without the need to pay the Union Pacific Railroad to relocate its line to the north. One cannot conceive of any circumstance that would cause Simon Benson, the first chairman of the highway commission, or Oswald West, the Oregon governor who appointed him, to approve the mindless destruction of this unique, creative work.

In 1908, the United States government established the Oregon National Forest of 14,000 acres between Warrendale and Viento. In 1915, after the completion of the Multnomah County portion of the Columbia River Highway, the U.S. Forest Service established its first campground at Eagle Creek. Samuel Lancaster promoted a trail system, and trails were started up Wahkeena, Multnomah, Eagle and Herman Creeks. To prevent the Corps of Engineers from using Beacon Rock as a source of rock for ocean jetties, a resident, Henry Biddle, purchased the landmark. Biddle's heirs attempted to give the landmark to the State of Washington, but Governor Roland Hartley turned them down, saying the gift amounted to a form of tax evasion. John Ainsworth intervened and urged the heirs to sell the monolith to the State of Oregon for $1.00. However, Washington's incoming Governor Clarence Martin accepted the gift and Beacon Rock is now a Washington State Park.

The Cascade Rapids, where the Columbia River drops 37 feet in 4 miles, were an impediment to river traffic, not only to Lewis and Clark, but to the settlers who followed. The rapids divide the Columbia River into the lower river (to the estuary), and middle river (to Celilo Falls). Until the Barlow Toll Road was built, settlers took to the river on rafts or bateaux to complete the final leg of their arduous trip to the Willamette Valley. The Cascade Indians, acting as porters, assisted settlers in making the portage around the rapids, which activity provided them with an income. In 1850, Francis A. Chenowith filed for a donation land claim on the north shore and, in 1851 started building a rail line. Motive power was provided by mule teams, which pulled a cart along the line that had dimensional timbers laid down as rail. This portage line was sold to Daniel and Putnam Bradford, who extended the line to below the lower cascades and named the enterprise the Cascade Railroad. A settlement grew around the portage that included a sawmill, worker quarters, a store and a blockhouse, Fort Rains (1855), for security. That same year, another blockhouse, Fort Cascades, was built. In 1856, a detachment under Major Lugenbeck constructed a third blockhouse at the upper Cascades.

This portage line had displaced the Indian porters, which may have caused resentment to build. This, together with other grievances, led the natives to react. In 1856, the Yakama tribe, abetted by Cascade Indians, attacked a work crew at a trestle. The attack started a running battle between portage workers and the attacking warriors along the rail line. Two workers were killed before the balance of the crew gained the protection of the blockhouse. Settlers were also attacked. Mr. and Mrs. Erastus Joslyn escaped to The Dalles aboard the steamer, *Mary*, though their home was burned. The Indians burned the Bradford Mill and other buildings. Armed settlers gathered at the blockhouse to keep the attackers at bay and summoned help. Lt. Phil Sheridan brought troopers from Fort Vancouver and Colonel George Wright, bound for Spokane, reversed direction to respond to the threat. Sheridan's troops together with a detachment under Lt. Colonel Edward Steptoe launched a coordinated attack that caused the Yakamas to flee and the locals to surrender. Lt. Sheridan hanged several Cascade Indians after the battle. The war lasted until 1858.

In 1858, J.O. Van Bergen started a competing line on the south shore from Bonneville to the upper Cascades. He soon sold out to Colonel Joseph Ruckel and H. Olmstead, who completed the Oregon Portage Railroad. Both lines competed for the trade provided by steamboat traffic. Steamboats would unload passengers and cargo either at the western or the eastern terminals of each line. The freight and passengers were then transported around the rapids to be reloaded for passage up or down the river. In 1862, Colonel Ruckel brought Oregon's first locomotive, the Oregon Pony, to power the train transporting goods between Bonneville and Cascade Locks. Built by Vulcan Iron Works, San Francisco, the Pony pulled an average of 200 tons of freight every day during the two years it operated. The discovery of gold at Orofino, Washington Territory, and in the Blue Mountains of Oregon increased traffic significantly, and the "Pony" line prospered. However, by the early-1860s, John C. Ainsworth's Oregon Steam Navigation Company (OSN) had established a monopoly over Columbia River steamboat traffic. For a time, the OSN patronized one line then the other to keep rates low, but decided to enhance its monopoly by buying the Cascade Railroad for $155,000. Unable to compete, Ruckel also sold the Oregon Portage Railroad to the Company, giving the latter total control of river traffic. By 1865, the OSN had 29 steamships, 13 schooners, 4 barges, the two portages at the Cascade Rapids and a portage railroad around Celilo Falls.

The salmon runs that helped support the native population also attracted settlers who had ideas for exploitation of the resource. In 1879, Sam Wilson built a fishwheel at the Cascades. Frank Warren, who built a cannery at Warrendale, leased Bradford Island and installed several fishwheels in the area. His cannery processed the catch, and other fishermen, with fishwheels, seines and gillnet boats, supplied canneries at Dodson and Rooster Rock. Gillnetters operated out of Corbett Landing, Dalton Point and other locales; a seine fishery at Rooster Rock used horses to tail the net; and fishwheels lined the river at many locations.

In 1864, President Abraham Lincoln signed an Act of Congress creating the Northern Pacific Railroad Company. In 1869, Congress chartered the Northern Pacific Railroad (NPRR), with a mandate to complete a rail line across the northern states and terminate in either Seattle or Portland. John Ainsworth, realizing the effect a railraod might have on the Oregon Steam Navigation Company (OSN), lobbied to have the NPRR connect with the OSN system through the Columbia River Gorge. He sold the OSN to the NPRR, which promptly went bankrupt. Ainsworth then bought back the OSN. In 1879, Henry Villard, at the behest of a group of German investors, had come to the Northwest to investigate the financial dealings of Ben Holladay of the Oregon and California Railroad (O & C). Villard gained control of the O & C, and then, in a series of transactions, also gained control of the OSN. Villard renamed the company the Oregon Railroad and Navigation Company (OR & N). Because the NPRR had experienced financial difficulties, he was also able to gain control of the Northern Pacific. Next he proceeded to connect the OR & N line to the westward bound Northern Pacific. He completed the track through the Gorge in 1882 and by September, 1883, the transcontinental line opened. Meanwhile, in 1878, the U.S. Congress authorized the construction of a lock at the Cascades to permit riverboats to pass the rapids. Construction commenced in 1879, but the Army Corps of Engineers did not complete the job until 1896. Thus, two major impediments to transportation through the Gorge, the Cascade Rapids and the mountainous topography had, by 1896, been overcome for river and train traffic. However, the narrows and Celilo Falls continued to impede river traffic from the "middle" to the "upper" river.

Hood River County, the final county carved from Wasco County in 1908, is bounded on the west by the crest of the Cascade Mountains, on the north by the Columbia River and, on the east and south, by Wasco County. The town of Cascade Locks supplanted the Cascade Indian tribal village of Cathleyackty. The abundant food source plus river-bound trade enabled the native population to live in permanent villages. When Lewis and Clark passed through here, Clark described the Indian lodges: "...The houses [are] similar to those described [at the narrows], with this difference only, that they are larger, say from 35 to 50 feet by 30 feet, raised about 5 feet above the earth, and nearly as much below...[The] houses are calculated for four, five, and six families, each family having a nice painted ladder to ascend up to their beds. I saw in those houses several wooden images all cut in imitation of men, but differently fashioned and placed in the most conspicuous parts of the houses, probably as an ornament." The explorers noted, however, that some lodges had been abandoned. Undoubtedly, this was a consequence of the introduction of smallpox by a trading vessel, which disease had decimated the native population of the lower river.

The Oregon Portage Railroad

These 1867 C.E. Watkins photographs show the portage line along the Oregon shoreline across from Bradford Island.

The Upper Cascades

The Upper Cascades, 1909 (Table Mountain in background). The Cascade Rapids hindered navigation on the Columbia River until locks were completed in 1896.

Photo, the author's collection.

The Cascade Rapids

Two sternwheelers approach the Cascade Locks.   *Photo postcard, the author.*

An Artist's Rendition of the Bridge of the Gods

Artist Fred Routledge's idea of the final appearance of the Bridge of the Gods (under construction, completed in 1926). After completion of the bridge, Charlie Smith's ferry, Eva Jane, *that operated between Stevenson and Cascade Locks, ceased operation.*

Print, the author's collection.

Cascade Locks (The Town)

The Columbia River Highway became the main street through the town of Cascade Locks. This late '30s (or early '40s) photograph shows Main Street at the time.

Photo postcard courtesy of Steve Lehl.

184

Penn's Tavern and Cabins, Cascade Locks

Penn's business complex was located along the CRH east of Cascade Locks.

Photo postcard courtesy of Carol Royse.

The CRH East of Cascade Locks

CRH east of Cascade Locks (approaching Herman Creek). Quarry Island shown became a source for rock used for many purposes on the River, including jetties. A nearby industrial area may become the "home" for a gambling casino.

Oregon Highway Commission photo courtesy of Dennis Wiancko.

Shellrock Mountain

CRH at the base of Shellrock Mountain. Later, a stone wall was built to contain rock fall. The talus slope of Shellrock Mountain was a barrier to a road through the Gorge for years.

Oregon Highway Commission (OHC) photo courtesy of Dennis Wiancko.

CRH between Shellrock Mountain and Starvation Creek

The CRH east of Shellrock Mountain took travelers through a spectacular section along the river.   *Photo postcard courtesy of Steve Lehl.*

Lindsey Creek Inn

Lindsey Creek Inn, milepost 56, CRH near Starvation Creek.

Photo postcard courtesy of Steve Lehl.

Half-Tunnel Near Mitchell Point   West Approach, Mitchell Point

Construction details, CRH near Mitchell Point, Hood River County.

Left, OHC photo courtesy of Dennis Wiancko; right photo courtesy of Steve Lehl.

West Portal, Mitchell Point Tunnel

The spectacular viaduct approach to the Mitchell Point Tunnel, constructed in 1915.

Photo, artist Charles W. Post.

A View of the Mitchell Point Tunnel from the River

Samuel Lancaster: The tunnel at Mitchell Point "is fully equal to the famous Axenstrasse of Switzerland and one of the great features of the highway." Dynamited by the State of Oregon in 1966.　　　　　　　*Photo postcard courtesy of Steve Lehl.*

188

Mitchell Point Tunnel, Unexcelled!!

Conceived by Samuel Lancaster and Sam Hill and designed by John Elliott, the tunnel at Mitchell Point became one of the more famous landmarks on the CRH. Its destruction by the State of Oregon in 1966 is incomprehensible. Friends of the Historic Columbia Highway, a newly formed organization, have, as a goal, the replacement of the irreplacable by 2016.

Photos courtesy of Dave Sell and George Perry VI, respectively.

M.E. White's Mitchell Point Store

White's store catered to travelers on the CRH.   *Photo postcard courtesy of Steve Lehl.*

Ruthton Point

The CRH and viaduct at Ruthton Point, on the (west) approach of the highway to Hood River.
OHC photo courtesy of Dennis Wiancko.

Hood River County - Hood River and Vicinity

On May 27, 1918, the Oregon State Highway Commission let a contract to G.E. Kibbe to pave the 22.11 mile section of the Columbia River Highway from Cascade Locks to Hood River. Because of difficulties encountered in the Ruthton Hill section, the commission awarded a contract to re-grade and re-gravel that area. Because of this delay and other problems, Kibbe did not complete the contract until August 2, 1920. This contract included building guard fences, parapet walls and rubble masonry walls. Also in 1918, the Oregon State Highway Commission awarded a contract to Parker and Banfield for the construction of a bridge across Hood River. Completed that year, the structure cost $49,300.66. C.E. Carter, resident engineer, Hood River County, supervised the construction of the Hood River Bridge. Supported by three arch spans of 95-feet each, the 395-foot bridge spanned Hood River. In 1920, the Columbia River Highway, Cascade Locks to Hood River, was paved.

On January 7, 1919, the highway commission awarded a contract to grade a 1.37-mile section of the Columbia River Highway east of Hood River. This section came to be known as the Hood River Loops. On the same date, the commission issued a contract to grade an additional 2.7 miles beyond the loops to the Wasco County line. On September 9, 1919, the State Highway Commission issued a contract to gravel 6.37 miles of the Columbia River Highway between Hood River and Mosier. This section presented some problems to engineers, because of the terrain and because of the O W R and N. tracks below, which hampered blasting and other work. The terrain necessitated boring two tunnels, the Twin Tunnels, in the Wasco County portion of the section. However, in 1920, the section opened to traffic, which meant, essentially, that a year-around highway through to eastern Oregon was open. Paving of this section was completed in 1922.

Newton Clark surveyed much of the Hood River Valley. His son, William L. Clark, became a civil engineer and helped his father with the survey of the railroad through the Gorge. William Clark also helped with the engineering of the Northern Pacific Railroad's tunnel through Stampede Pass in Washington's Cascade Mountains. From 1903 to 1907, young Clark worked as an engineer for Kiernan and Taylor at Cascade Locks. In 1907, he returned to Hood River where he became involved in the grain and milling business. When the CRH came through Hood River County, the state highway department hired Clark to work on the highway, which employment continued until 1922. That year he became, by appointment, city engineer of Hood River. In 1889, he had married Estella Mabee and the couple's son, Newton (named for his grandfather) graduated from Stanford University. Continuing in the family tradition, young Newton also became a surveyor and an engineer.

Robert Rand crossed the plains by wagon in 1859, experiencing many adventures on the trek. A severe storm brought a deluge with high winds, overturning several wagons. When the weather improved, the sun soon dried the track so that the movement of oxen, wagons, horses and men raised so much dust that Robert, interviewed by Fred Lockley of the *Oregon Journal* said, "I swallowed enough dust by the time we got to Fort Laramie to make several good sized men." The wagon train turned to Salt Lake where a woman, Mrs. Martin, who had lost her husband, implored the emigrants to take her with them to California. The widow and her two daughters had become prospective brides in the Mormon community and wished to avoid the proposed matches. Hiding the three in a wagon, the emigrants left Salt Lake City. The refugees remained hidden during a confrontation between the emigrants and five Mormon men who came looking for the widow and her daughters. The party finally obtained help from a few U.S.

Army troopers who happened along. The emigrants' tribulations had not ended. When they camped at the foot of the Sierra Nevada Range, they were robbed by a man they had befriended.

After mining in California for 3 years, Rand returned to Wisconsin, then moved to Iowa, where he remained until he came to Oregon in 1884. He landed at The Dalles and encountered a man who recommended that he consider Hood River. In Hood River, he purchased fifty acres for $1,200. He told Lockley, "The town of Hood River later spread all over my place and after [being platted the property] sold for ninety-five thousand dollars." Rand continued buying and selling parcels, explaining, "Whenever I [could] make a profit on a place I let it go." In 1855, Rand bought the Mt. Hood Hotel, which he operated until 1893, selling it to C.A. Bell. He had also opened a store that he operated with his son, J.E. Rand. He sold this store and, in 1904, for $2800, purchased forty-three acres at the west end of Hood River. There he built the Wau-gwin-gwin Hotel. Rand operated the hotel until he sold the business to Portland lumberman and hotel owner, Simon Benson.

Benson engaged architect Morris Whitehouse to design a new hotel, which was built on the property and which opened on June 21, 1921. Italian stonemasons, who had constructed the stonework found on the new Columbia River Highway, built the stone walls, bridges and other stonework on the site. When business declined during the Depression years of the 1930s, the Neighbors of Woodcraft purchased the facility to use as a retirement home. Restoration of the hotel, started in 1977, continues to the present (2005). Now operated by the Columbia Gorge Hotel Company, the facility attracts tourists and others who have a taste for vintage elegance. The historic hotel is listed on the National Register of Historic Places.

Many early settlers had an impact on the history of Hood River County. A brief account of several follow. Included among settlers who established businesses in Hood River was Samuel F. Blythe, who arrived in Hood River in 1877. He purchased 22 acres west of the city and later bought another 21 acres. A printer by trade, he purchased the Hood River *Glacier* in 1894, which newspaper he controlled for about ten years. Blythe sold the newspaper to A.D. Moe after which he established the Twin Oaks Fruit Farm. A future hotel operator, Charles E. Bell, came to Hood River in 1890 to work for the Oregon Lumber Company. As foreman of the company's logging camp, he directed the logging of several thousand acres of timber from the foothills surrounding Mt. Hood. In 1893, he purchased the Mt. Hood Hotel, which he operated for approximately 8 years until it was sold to C.L. Gilbert. Bell returned to the logging business until 1907, when he re-purchased the hotel. In 1912, Bell made extensive improvements, adding a brick annex of forty rooms and renovating the original building.

In 1890, Samuel E. Bartmess moved to Hood River with his wife, Elda (Crouse). A merchant and an undertaker, he opened a furniture store and a mortuary. In 1892, Bartmess purchased a lot on Oak Street, where he erected a new building for his business. Bartmess helped found the Mazamas, a mountaineering club now headquartered in Portland. He participated in the organization's summit climb of Mt. Hood, thus becoming a charter member. In 1891, Framptom C. Brosius, M.D., purchased the medical practice of Dr. Thomas, which included a drug store. Dr. Brosius served in the medical corps of the Oregon National Guard, which, in 1898, was mobilized for duty in the Spanish-American War. He served with distinction in The Philippine Islands, participating in twenty-eight engagements. Dr. Brosius remained active in the Oregon National Guard, retiring in 1922 with the rank of Major. He practiced medicine in the valley from 1891 until his retirement, except for four years, 1923-1927, when he practiced in Elgin, Oregon. Dr. Brosius served several terms as a member of the Hood River city council, and two terms as mayor.

In 1899, another business man, E.R. Bradley, a printer by trade, moved to Hood River with his wife, Sarah A. (Lamon). He leased the Hood River *Sun*, which he published before opening a print shop and book store. In 1905, he started publishing a weekly, the Hood River *Newsletter*, which endeavor he continued for three years. Between 1908 and 1915, Bradley and his brother owned and operated a concrete contracting business. Bradley sold his interest in this enterprise to his brother and returned to the printing trade. In the early 1870s, Leonard Frank came to Oregon where he operated his father's sawmill in what became the Oak Grove District. His father also taught him the harness and saddle trade. In 1876, five years after his father had returned to Illinois, Frank sold the sawmill. He moved to The Dalles, where he established a prosperous business making saddles, harnesses and other leather goods. His son, Sherman J. Frank, learned the trade and, in 1903, moved to Hood River, where he opened his own saddle and harness shop. However, his timing was not propitious and, in 1909, he purchased an orchard. In 1915, he sold the orchard and moved to a 12-acre place on Belmont Road. There he established a herd of purebred Guernsey dairy cattle and distributed milk in the county. He also became a distributor of explosives in Eastern Oregon for the Dupont Company. (Which, given the extensive construction of roads then taking place, was a more propitious move.)

At age 16, Harry A. Hackett started working on sternwheelers on the Willamette and Columbia rivers. During the fourteen years he spent on steamboats, he advanced, obtaining both his engineer's and captain's licenses. For a time he worked as a fireman on an O R & N locomotive and happened to be on the train that became stranded in the Gorge for twenty-one days during the big storm of 1884-85. In 1888, Harry Hackett married Margaret E. Darling, daughter of H.L. Darling, wood finisher who worked on steamboats and other vessels. The couple had two children, Henry and Lavina. In 1891, Hackett purchased 80 acres in the Hood River Valley, of which he cleared about 20 acres, planting an orchard. In 1905, he moved into Hood River, but, in 1922, re-located to a small ranch in the valley. Hackett's son, Henry, married Mildred Metcalf of Hood River. Henry became a civil engineer and served as county roadmaster for Clatsop County, where he conducted a reconnaissance survey for a portion of the CRH from Portland to Seaside. Subsequently, the state highway department employed him as a resident engineer and later as personnel director. He and Mildred had three children, Mel, Helen and Russell. Harry and Margaret Hackett's daughter, Lavina, married James Holden of Lake Oswego. She and James had two children, Beryl and Edward. (For further information regarding Margaret Darling, see "Margaret Henderson," p. 88.)

Many other early settlers in the Hood River Valley planted orchards, which contributed greatly toward establishing the valley's reputation as one of the nation's premier fruit-producing regions. Milton D. Odell, born in 1863 on his father's preemptive claim of 160 acres, attended Wasco Academy in The Dalles. His father, William Odell, had settled in the valley in 1861. In addition to Odell's claim, he purchased another 50 acres on which he grew hay, a truck garden and ran cattle. Later, he planted fruit orchards. After completing school, Milton purchased 80 acres of timber near Odell, cleared the land and planted a fruit orchard and other farm crops. The town of Odell takes its name from the family. Another orchardist, John B. Jackson, native to the valley, attended the Pine Grove School. Upon reaching a majority, he took up a homestead south of his father's place and cleared about 70 acres, of which 22 acres were planted to an orchard and the remainder, pasture. He served as county road supervisor for nine years.

In 1875, Hans Lage purchased the 160-acre homestead of Milton Neal, situated about 4 miles south of Hood River. He and his sons cleared the land where they planted an orchard and garden crops and where they also raised chickens, cows and hogs. Lage made sausage and cured meat, which products he sold in Wasco County. Later he planted more land to orchards and developed a dairy herd of registered Jerseys. His three sons, Edward, George and Charles Lage, took an active part in managing the various farm and other enterprises. Hans Lage served as a county road supervisor for twenty years. Another orchardist, William F. Foss, moved from

Portland to Wasco County with his wife, Phoebe (Purser) Foss in 1877 and filed a homestead claim in the Hood River Valley. He cleared about 50 acres most of which he planted to fruit trees. One of the couple's five children, William Foss Jr., continued the family's orchard business.

In 1884, William H. Edick moved to the Hood River Valley where he purchased a 30-acre orchard. Later, he served as a deputy county assessor for 6 years and, in 1923, was appointed sheriff. In 1924, county voters elected him to the office. In 1892, a Wasco County "transplant," Charles Davis, who had developed a section of land near Dufur, sold that ranch and purchased 280 acres of the former Jesse Neal donation claim. He cleared the place and planted an orchard. In 1923, he sold the place to his son, Aubrey N. Davis. For years, a large spring on the Davis place provided water for Odell. Another orchardist, Louis Plog, came to the valley in 1902 and bought 90 acres of land south of Hood River, of which about 25 acres was in fruit trees. He planted more orchards, developing a valuable farm. His son, J.E. Plog, bought 34-plus acres of the old Peter Neal donation land claim, which he planted to apples, pears and cherries. He became a director of the Hood River Apple Growers Association and a director of the East Fork Irrigation District.

In 1903, C.H. Sletton came to Hood River, working first as a farm hand before becoming a clerk at the Bragg Mercantile Company. In 1910, he started working for the Apple Growers Association. Upon its formal establishment in 1913, he became the association's treasurer. The organization had few assets, but borrowed $5000 to buy a cold storage plant and to lease other facilities that were used to further the interests of its members. In 1926, the association, with 700 active members, grossed nearly $4 million dollars shipping apples, pears, cherries, strawberries and other fruit across the country; some to international customers. In the early 1900s, Martin M. Hill bought 50 acres in the valley, mostly timber and brush. He cleared the land and planted an apple orchard. Later, he removed the apple trees to plant pears. In 1912, Hill, with other local growers, erected an apple storage plant at Van Horn, which he managed for several years. It was later sold to the Hood River Apple Growers Association. When Hood River County separated from Wasco County in 1908, Hill became a member of the Board of County Commissioners. He also served as president of the Hood River State Bank for eight years.

"S Curves," CRH

The "S Curves" are near Inspiration Point. Photo postcard courtesy of Steve Lehl.

In 1905, James R. Nunamaker with his wife, Mary E. (Morgan) Nunamaker, moved their family to Hood River from Heppner, where he had operated a sheep ranch. He purchased 35 acres of the old Armstrong homestead west of Hood River and planted the place to apples, cherries and Anjou pears. In 1916, he purchased another 40 acres of orchard land in the Pine Grove District to which he later added 160 acres, concentrating on growing pears. Two of the couple's sons became associated with their parents in the orchard business and, in 1926, the Nunamakers packed and shipped more than 100,000 boxes of cherries, pears and apples. James Nunamaker became a director of the Hood River Apple Growers Association. He passed away in 1927, his wife having pre-deceased him. His sons continued the orchard business started by their father.

The Columbia Gorge Hotel

Simon Benson's Columbia Gorge Hotel, Hood River (designed by Morris H. Whitehouse), 1921.
Photo courtesy of George Perry VI.

The City of Hood River ca 1950

Identifiable business establishments include (left): Young's Bakery, Rexall Drugs and the Mt. Hood Hotel; Right: Eby's Food Store, Hood River Market, Kier's Drugs, Apple Blossom Cafe, Hackett's Furniture, Gabel's Books and Gifts, Marshall Wells and a Chevrolet dealer.
Photo postcard courtesy of Steve Lehl.

CRH, Hood River (looking west) ca 1937

CRH, Hood River, Oregon, mid '30s. Business establishments include (left), Moore Electric, the Stag and a drug store; right, Tebbs Coffee Shop, Mt. Hood Hotel, Dude's Tobacco and Candy, a drug store and J.C. Penney. Photo postcard courtesy of Steve Lehl.

Hotel Oregon, Hood River, Oregon

The landmark Hotel Oregon located on the CRH in Hood River.

Photo postcard, the author.

The Hood River Bridge

Parker and Banfield Company built this 404-foot, 3-arch bridge across the Hood River in 1918. It cost $49,300.66. The destruction of this bridge prompted a movement to save the remaining segments of the historic Columbia River Highway   *Photo courtesy of David Sell.*

Hood River Loops - Interstate Bridge

The Hood River loops climb the point east of Hood River toward Mosier. The interstate bridge opened in December, 1924.   *Photo courtesy of Steve Lehl.*

197

Inspiration Point

Inspiration Point, Hood River County.   *Photo postcard courtesy of Steve Lehl.*

Inspiration Point, 2005

Inspiration Point, on the Historic CRH, can be reached from a trailhead east of Hood River, or from Mosier.   *Photo, the author.*

Wasco County

The Columbia River Highway: On January 7, 1919, a contract for the construction of the section from the Hood River County line to Mosier was let, which involved completing the Twin Tunnels. The terrain in this section created many problems for the contractor amplified by the O W R & N. Company's rail line paralleling the highway some 300-feet below. Rock conditions and the apparent movement of hillsides in the vicinity caused frequent rock falls, which foretold of future problems. The firm, A.D. Kern Company, completed this contract in 1920. Construction of the bridge across Mosier Creek, designed by Conde B. McCullough, started in 1920 with a completion date set for January 1, 1921. The firm, Lindstrom and Feigenson, successfully bid and completed the job on time. The bridge, with a center arch span of 110 feet and two 36-foot approaches (182 feet) cost approximately $47,400. On October 7, 1919, a contract was awarded for grading an approximate 9-mile section from Mosier to Rowena. About six miles east of Mosier, the highway crossed a deep ravine necessitating a 75-foot arch span with two 15-foot approaches, all of reinforced concrete construction. Conde B. McCullough also designed this beautiful, arch span. Because of what the highway commission considered excessive bid proposals, state workers completed the project. Another contract was let for grading the section between Rowena and Chenowith Creek. Contracts to surface these sections with gravel were awarded in 1920. Both sections were paved in 1922.

In 1919, the Highway Department graded the 7.76 section from Rowena to The Dalles and spanned Chenowith Creek with a reinforced concrete bridge. In May, 1919, the 2.1 mile section from Chenowith to The Dalles was paved, with Wasco County paying a portion of the cost. In 1917, Wasco County had graded the section of the Columbia River Highway from The Dalles to Seufert. On March 26, 1919, the highway commission let a contract to pave this section, which was completed in August, 1919. The bridge over the Deschutes River, completed in June, 1920, replaced a toll ferry in use since 1867. The 12.5 mile highway section from Seufert to the Deschutes River bridge required a 210-foot bridge over 5-Mile Creek and two railroad overpasses. This section, when completed, opened the Columbia River Highway from Pendleton to the sea. By 1922, the highway, from Astoria to 5-Mile Creek east of The Dalles, was paved. At an observance held on June 7, 1922 near Rowena, Simon Benson ceremoniously spread the last bit of Warrenite that completed the paving of the highway from Astoria to 5-Mile Creek. The highway beyond 5-Mile Creek to Pendleton, though not paved, had been graveled.

Wasco County: On January 11, 1854, the Oregon Territorial Legislature created Wasco County. The county included all of what is now Eastern Oregon from the crest of the Cascade Mountains eastward. It also included the southern part of what is now the State of Idaho between the 42nd and 46th parallels, and stretched into what became the states of Montana and Wyoming. It encompassed approximately 130,000 square miles, the largest county established in the history of the country. One of the first orders of business facing the newly appointed Wasco County Commission, Chairman W.C. Laughlin and Commissioners Warren Keith and John Tompkins, was acting upon applications from three individuals to operate ferries: Orlando Humison, on the Snake River below Fort Boise; Richard Marshall, on the Snake River near Salmon Falls; and C.E. Irvine, on the Green River in what is now Wyoming.

The site that became The Dalles was established by the Townsite Act. Incorporated as Dalles City in 1857, the United States Post Office Department changed the name to The Dalles to avoid confusion with Dallas, Oregon. At the time of its incorporation, Dalles City had six dry goods stores, two saloons, three blacksmith shops, four boarding houses, a meat market and a

Wasco County - 1854

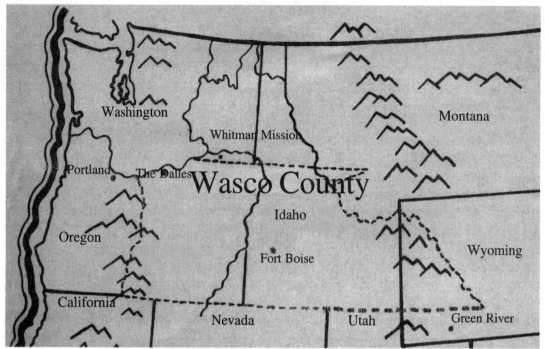

Illustration by Jeanne Becharas [modified]. From Shadows of Yesterday *by Marshall Nelson,
The Dalles Optimist Printer, 1954.*

livery stable. When Oregon became a state on February 14, 1859, Wasco County lost that portion of its area lying outside Oregon's eastern boundary. Subsequently, the county would lose more of its territory as the Oregon Legislature created other counties east of the Cascade Mountains.

The Indian Wars, precipitated by various factors, started in 1847 with the Whitman massacre. The Homestead Act brought more settlers and a concomitant increase in hostility from native Americans. Indian tribes likely resented the encroachment by whites on lands they considered theirs. In response to Indian attacks, the Territorial Legislature authorized the formation of the Oregon Volunteers, who arrived at The Dalles in 1848, took over the vacated Wascopan Mission and named it Fort Wascopan. The first regular U.S. Army troops established Camp Drum in 1850, which became Fort Drum and, shortly thereafter, Fort Dalles. Lt. Sylvester Mowry described The Dalles as "the most desolate place, with nothing to recommend it except wolves, coyotes, rattlesnakes and skunks." In 1852, a contingent of troops including Major Granville O. Haller, accompanied by his family and his children's nanny, Mary Pigott, sailed from New York, crossed the Isthmus to the Pacific and continued the voyage by ship to San Francisco. In 1853, the troops landed at Fort Vancouver, where some were sent to Seattle; some to Fort Dalles. During the Indian Wars, particularly from 1855 to 1858, Fort Dalles served as an important outpost during the crucial period when the U.S. Army garrison and volunteer forces engaged various tribes in battle. The Fort provided a haven for settlers who fled their homes during the conflicts and its troopers helped emigrants who traveled along the Oregon Trail. In 1858, according to the *Oregon Statesman*, The Dalles was "one of the important towns of Oregon...The buildings and all the improvements are of the best and most substantial character, and the garrison is said to be the most comfortable one on the Pacific [Coast]." In 1859, soldiers at Fort Dalles published *The Dalles Journal*, which eventually became the *Weekly Mountain-*

eer. After the Civil War started, the War Department called the U.S. Army garrison east, and the fort declined in importance. In 1905, the federal government transferred title of the fort to the Oregon Historical Society.

In 1860, the discovery of gold at Orofino, Washington Territory, and at locales in Wasco County brought prospectors, miners and others to the diggings. The Dalles became an important transportation hub and supply center for the mines. In 1863, the Oregon Steam and Navigation Company completed a railroad from The Dalles to Celilo to handle the increase in freight. Rates were so high that the company paid for its new steamer, the *Okanagan*, on her first trip. J. Conser & Sons flour and seed store added mining outfits to its stock and the Globe Hotel provided rooms for gold seekers. The prosperity engendered by the discovery of gold hastened the growth of The Dalles, and gave the city added importance as a supply center. By 1863, the population of The Dalles exceeded 5000 persons. In 1866, in response to the boom, Billy Wiley, a settler who had been operating the toll bridge across the Deschutes River, started freighting between The Dalles and Canyon City. However, when the mining boom ended, the population remained static and, by 1900, had actually declined. By 1920, the population, at 5807, finally surpassed the level reached in the city's early years.

In 2004, *The Dalles Chronicle* published *Wasco County*, a sequiscentennial history of Wasco County, which documents significant historical events concerning the county. The book, edited by Dan Spatz, is a "must read" for anyone interested in the history of The Dalles and Wasco County. The book cites the following events:

In 1864, the Sisters of the Holy Name established St. Mary's Academy as a Catholic high school for girls. In 1865, Congress appropriated $125,000 to build a U.S. Mint in The Dalles, but the need for the facility had disappeared before it was completed. The building subsequently became a warehouse. Robert Penland established the first flour mill in The Dalles in 1866. In 1870, Ingwert C. Nickelsen opened a book store on First Street, which continues to operate as a bookstore to the present. Another inveterate business is the Baldwin Saloon, which opened in 1876. In 1884, the Seufert Brothers, Frank and Theodore, purchased the Whitcomb Cannery and fishwheel at Big Eddy. The brothers added more fishwheels and incorporated the business in 1891. By 1896, the cannery produced 1,500 cases of salmon or fruit daily. The cannery became a landmark along the Columbia River, and operated for decades. In 1888, a light plant, First Electric Light, opened at a location on Seventh Street and Union. In 1890, *The Dalles Chronicle* printed its first edition. Also, area orchardists sent the first fresh fruit shipment from The Dalles. A Chinese restaurant, the Chin, opened at 310 East Second Street. Another Chinese restaurant [Canton Wok]operates at this same location at the present time [2004]. When the Corps of Engineers completed the locks at the Cascade Rapids in 1896, ocean-going ships could dock at The Dalles. In 1914, the new (third) Wasco County Courthouse at Fifth and Washington opened. In 1915, the U.S. Army Corps of Engineers completed the Celilo Canal, which put the portage from The Narrows beyond Celilo Falls out of business. In 1915, The Dalles School District completed a "fire proof" high school building, which, in 1940, a fire totally gutted. In 1916, prohibition closed 27 saloons in The Dalles. In 1917, the steamboat era came to a close with the transfer of the *Bailey Gatzert* to Puget Sound.

Several individuals had a significant role in the history of The Dalles and Wasco County. Two early storekeepers included Nathan Olney and Milo Cushing. Olney, who later became Wasco County's first Justice of the Peace, built a store at the mouth of Chenowith Creek that became known as Olney's Store. Milo Cushing, who came to Fort Dalles in 1852 with two companies of soldiers commanded by Captain Benjamin Alvord, opened a store on the river front after his discharge from the Army in 1853. The log building featured a hand-hewn counter fashioned from a large log. In 1854, Cushing married Mary Pigott and the couple became permanent residents of Wasco County, first living in the store. In 1856, Cushing was elected Treasurer of Wasco County. He had also served as postmaster of Fort Dalles for a brief period. After selling his business and other interests in The Dalles, the Cushing family eventually settled on a farm on Fifteenmile Creek, where they planted an orchard of pears, plums and peaches as well as a grape arbor. Of the seven Cushing children, only three, Milo, William and Elizabeth O., survived their parents.

Another early settler, Zenas F. Moody, came to Oregon in 1850 by way of Cape Horn. He settled in The Dalles and became involved in several business ventures involving his ownership of large warehouses. He conducted a commission business in wheat and handled ranch supplies under the name, Z.F. Moody Warehouse Company. In 1900, because of the growth of the company, Moody established a branch operation at Shaniko. In 1903, Shaniko wool sales reached three million pounds and, in 1904, five million pounds. The company bought and sold goods used or raised on area ranches, but dealt principally in wool and wheat. In 1883, Zenas F. Moody became Oregon's seventh governor. In 1886, he helped charter The Dalles National Bank and became an officer of the bank. He accumulated several thousand acres of land including a ranch that stretched approximately twelve miles from the mouth of the Deschutes River south along the east bank.

In 1893, the Moody Warehouse Company hired Dominick A. Anthony to work at its ranch at the mouth of the Deschutes River. Anthony may have been engaged because of his expertise with horses. According to family lore, he had been hired by Bill Cody's Wild West Show to care for and help train the show's horses. Anthony, an immigrant from Spain, had been living in Wasco County since 1884. In 1887, when he gained citizenship, he resided in Fossil, Oregon. His first wife, Martha (Redshaw) Anthony, died of "quick consumption" in 1889 and was interred in the Fossil cemetery. A grieving Anthony traveled to Iowa to tell his wife's parents of her demise; he remained there for some time. On November 29, Domonick Anthony married Elizabeth B. Redshaw, who returned with him to Fossil. In January, 1892, the couple's first child, Eble J. was born. The following year he took the job on the Moody ranch.

The Anthony family lived in a home provided for them on the ranch. Dominick Anthony's responsibilities included the operation of the company's ferry that transported goods, people and livestock across the Deschutes River. While living on the ranch, three more children were born to the couple: Loren F., in 1894, James A., in 1896 and Ena O., in 1899. (The fifth child, Fred A., was born in 1902.) When the Spanish-American War broke out, certain individuals in the immediate area started expressing hostility toward anyone of Spanish descent, specifically targeting Dominick Anthony. Governor Moody made it clear that any hostile action taken against his employee would not be tolerated. At the time, he urged Anthony to carry a gun and to shoot anyone who overtly threatened him. Needless to say, nothing came of the threat.

In 1900, Anthony worked to install a large waterwheel for an irrigation system in the creek that ran through the ranch. While working, he lost his footing, slipped into the creek and the waterwheel fell, pinning him to a cement foundation block. Seriously injured, he was moved to The Dalles to convalesce. After he regained some strength, he started working at Tackman's greenhouse in The Dalles. However, Anthony never fully recovered and passed away in 1904. Only four of the Anthony children survived childhood. In 1910, Eble married Elizabeth O. Cushing, daughter of Milo and Mary (Pigott) Cushing of Fifteenmile Creek. Eble and Elizabeth Anthony had a large family and many of their descendants live (or lived) in Wasco County. In

1913, Loren F. Anthony died in an accident at the Umatilla railroad depot, where he worked for the O W R & N. James Anthony died in the flu pandemic of 1918 and was interred in a cemetery in Corvallis, Oregon. In 1914, Ena Anthony married Clifford D. McNurlen of Umatilla, Oregon, but as far as known, the couple had no children. Eventually, Governor Moody's son, William H. Moody, purchased Moody Warehouse Company from his father and brothers and thereafter managed the business. He added the 5000-acre Bake Oven Ranch to the company's holdings, which gave it additional land for planting wheat and raising livestock.

Jonah H. Mosier came to Oregon from California in 1852. He had experience as a storekeeper, millright, blacksmith and carpenter. He settled in The Dalles that same year and built a store for Milo Cushing. He built several other structures including the town's first hotel. In 1854, Mosier and his wife, Jane, filed donation land claims of 320 acres each 16 miles west of The Dalles on what became Mosier Creek, where Mosier built a sawmill. The mill, operated by water power, produced the lumber that Mosier needed for his construction projects in The Dalles. Mosier transported his lumber up the Columbia River by scow. He built a landing for steamboats that came to be known as Mosier Landing. Fire destroyed the sawmill, which Mosier rebuilt. However, floods, particularly the flood of 1859, raised havoc, causing Mosier to quit the sawmill and construction businesses. He then went into the stock business, supplying horses to freighters and stage companies. He ran pack trains to mining districts and also drove cattle to the mining camps of Idaho and Montana. Mosier passed away in 1894, having accumulated more than 1,000 acres of land. That year, his son, Jefferson Mosier, platted what became the town of Mosier. He became the first president of the Mosier Valley Bank and founded the *Mosier Bulletin*. He built Mosier's first water system, which delivered running water to Mosier homesites. In 1905, the construction of a prune dryer and box factory gave the economy of Mosier a boost. Local farmers established the Mosier Fruit Growers Association in 1907. In 1912, C.A. Hage, who had settled in Mosier in 1901, purchased a 55-acre place and started a cider plant. In 1918, he added a press with a capacity of 2000 gallons per day (forty 50-gallon barrels). He gradually increased production until he sold, in 1925, 25,000 gallons of cider. He created a drink, half cider, half cranberry juice, that became very popular.

In 1859, Henry Klindt, stonemason, came by wagon train to The Dalles. He found work erecting some of the first stone structures in the city. In 1868, he filed on 54 acres situated west of The Dalles and added, by purchase, another 250 acres to his holdings. Here, he developed a truck-garden, but continued to practice his skills in laying stone. His son, Walter J. Klindt, became active in the fishing industry on the Columbia River. Another '59 settler, Levi Chrisman, moved to The Dalles from Dayton and leased a farm near Dufur, which he purchased in 1862. He sold the ranch, moved to The Dalles, became a dealer in grain and prospered. He married Mary A. Murphy, whose father was a circuit rider who brought the gospel to many isolated settlements in eastern Oregon. The couple had seven children. In 1890, two of their sons, Levi and Frank, opened a meat market in The Dalles and also dealt in livestock. In 1893, Levi (Jr.) married Edna C. Martin and the couple had 5 children. Elected Sheriff of Wasco County in 1906, Levi Chrisman Jr. served as sheriff for many years.

In 1862, John S. Schenck located in The Dalles, where he became an agent for the Oregon Steam Navigation Company. He operated in that capacity until 1883, when became a principal in establishing the banking house of Schenck & Bell, which he managed for two years. In 1885, he became the first president of the First National Bank, The Dalles, and served in that capacity until his death in 1913. In addition to his financial achievements, Mr. Schenck accumulated an approximate 1,200-acre ranch situated in Grass Valley. In 1863, Nicholas B. Sinnott and Dennis Handley leased the Umatilla House, owned by H.P. Isaacs of Walla Walla. The two purchased the hotel in 1865. Under the management of the two partners, the Umatilla House became the most popular hotel in eastern Oregon. In 1879, fire destroyed the original structure, which Sinnott and Handley soon replaced with a new building. Unfortunately, in May, 1879, the new Umatilla House also burned. Sinnott and Handley rebuilt and continued to operate the Umatilla House until their deaths; "Major" Handley died in 1891 and "Colonel" Sinnott, in 1897. Colonel Sinnott's son, Roger Sinnott, then managed the hotel. The Umatilla House was demolished in 1929. Another of the Colonel's sons, Nicholas J. Sinnott, represented the second District in Congress from 1912-1928.

Fred W. Wilson, though born in Ohio in 1872, always considered himself a native son of Oregon. His father, Judge Joseph G. Wilson, a resident of The Dalles, had been elected to Congress in 1872, and moved his family east to serve. Unfortunately, Judge Wilson died in 1873, and Fred's mother, Elizabeth Wilson, returned to Oregon with her four children. President Ulysses Grant appointed Mrs. Wilson postmaster at The Dalles, a unique honor for a woman at that time, and she served as postmaster for twelve years. Young Fred Wilson obtained his first employment as a purser aboard the steamer, *Regulator*, and also served as purser on the *Dalles City*. His mother "resigned" Fred from the latter position so that he would study law. He studied with Huntington and Wilson, passed the bar exam and became a practicing attorney, taking up the profession in 1896. In 1908, he received an appointment to the circuit court. In 1924, members of the State Bar Association of Oregon elected Fred Wilson their president.

In 1881, Peter J. Stadelman came to The Dalles with his parents, Joseph and Mary Stadelman. His father leased the Catholic mission land claim of 640 acres, which he farmed and later purchased. Peter J. attended a public school in The Dalles until he became a newsboy for *The Oregonian* at age twelve. Postmaster and Mayor Michael Nolan also hired Stadelman to work in the post office, where he became deputy postmaster before his 16th birthday. In 1893, Stadelman opened a fruit and vegetable store at The Dalles, which he enlarged the following year. That winter, he cut and stored ice from a nearby lake and sold it during the summer. In 1898, the business became a wholesale and retail fruit and ice company in which Peter Stadelman owned two-thirds and his brother, Joseph, one-third. The firm bought and shipped fruit throughout the United States and also handled coal, wood and ice. In 1907, the brothers purchased their father's farm. In 1909, the company built an ice plant followed shortly by a cold storage building with facilities for storing apples. In 1918, voters elected Peter J. Stadelman as Mayor of The Dalles, a position he held for many years. In 1920, Peter Stadelman helped organize the Citizens National Bank and was made its president. In 1924, he and N.A. Bonn became partners in a hardware business. In 1925, Joseph Stadelman withdrew from the company, leaving Peter Stadelman in control. The Stadelman firm shipped cherries, peaches, pears, apricots, strawberries, apples and vegetables in large quantities throughout the United States and abroad.

Ladru Barnum was born in 1877 on the Wasco County homestead of his father, Henry Barnum, that became the townsite of Moro. His father had sailed around Cape Horn and settled in the county. Ladru Barnum attended the school started (and funded) by his father after which he completed a business course in Portland. He was employed as a clerk before taking a job with the Wasco Warehouse and Milling Company as a grain buyer and field man. For 20 years he worked in that capacity and also managed the firm's bank. In 1919, he became vice-president and general manager of the First National Bank of The Dalles. He also served as vice-president of the Bank of Moro, a director of the Bank of Wasco and a director of the Eastern Oregon Banking Company of Shaniko. Active in civic affairs, he served four terms as president of The Dalles Chamber of Commerce and acted as a district trustee of the Kiwanis Club.

Andrew Keller came to America in 1877, where he learned the bakery trade. In 1883, he located in The Dalles where the Newman Bakery employed him. Shortly thereafter, he opened his own shop, which he operated until 1907. After becoming involved in the operation of a brewery, he entered into a partnership with Charles Johnson to construct several structures in The Dalles, including the Wasco warehouse and elevators, a large flour mill and a new home for the First National Bank. He served on the city council and as a water commissioner. J.M. Patterson, Civil War veteran, settled in Salem, Oregon in 1869. In 1885, he obtained employment as a clerk on the Warm Springs Indian reservation. After serving there about a year, he moved to The Dalles to become a bookkeeper for the A.M. Williams Company, a position he held for 8 years. In 1894, the First National Bank employed him as cashier. Patterson became the postmaster of The Dalles in 1901 and served in that position until 1905. In 1908, he purchased a farm and established a cherry orchard, which he operated until 1927. In 1921, Patterson, age 76, was elected Treasurer of Wasco County; voters re-elected him in 1923 for another four years. J.P. McInerny journeyed to Oregon in 1874, located in The Dalles and obtained employment in the Max Vogt and Company store. In 1879 he became part owner of the firm, Herbering and McInerny, a store that handled dry goods exclusively. In addition to his business interests, McInerny served as a city commissioner, The Dalles.

In 1886, George E. Blakely, a trained pharmacist, obtained employment as a druggist with R.B. Hood. In January, 1887, Blakely purchased the drug store, which became affiliated with the Rexall Drug Store chain. In 1919, he helped organize the Wasco County Bank and became its first president. He also became a successful fruit grower, having established a 30-acre cherry orchard. He served on the city council, The Dalles, and later became a county judge of Wasco and Hood River Counties. He became the second president of the Oregon Pharmaceutical Association and served fifteen years on the Oregon State Board of Pharmacy.

In the early 1880s, when J.A. Fleck came to The Dalles, he worked in the machine shop of the Oregon Railroad and Navigation Company. In 1887, he took up a homestead on Chenowith Creek, land that he farmed until 1893, when he sold the property. Next he purchased 60 acres of the Catholic mission farm, where he planted grapes, the first attempt at commercializing grapes in eastern Oregon. His efforts brought him much recognition and many awards, including a silver medal at the 1904 World's Fair at St. Louis, Missouri. Mr. Fleck bought and sold a number of tracts of land, but continued to cultivate and care for his grapes.

J.P. Thomsen, who served an apprenticeship to learn the carpenter trade in California, journeyed to Spokane, Washington, in 1890 to help rebuild the city after a disastrous fire. In the fall of 1891, he ventured to The Dalles, which had also suffered a calamitous fire, to help in rebuilding the city. In partnership with Hans Hansen, he started a lumberyard and planing mill. The partners also did construction work and, in 1892, built the first section of The Dalles Hospital as well as homes for Judge Bennett, George Blakely and Dr. Rheinhart. The firm put up a large warehouse at The Dalles in sixty days. The partnership continued until 1908, when Thomsen moved to the Hood River valley, where he established both an orchard and a dairy of registered Jersey cattle. His interest in dairying caused him to help organize the Hood River Dairy Cooperative whose members elected him as its first president. He also took an active interest in the Pine Grove School District and supervised the construction of the district's new school. In addition to his other interests, Mr. Thomsen engaged in the real estate business in the valley.

Harry E. Greene, elected cashier of the Citizens National Bank when it opened in 1921, came to The Dalles in 1903 to manage the office of the Edward C. Pease Company. In 1905, he became a teller for the bank, French & Company, later advancing to the position of assistant cashier. Other officers of Citizens included P.J. Stadelman, president and Dr. J.A. Reuter, vice-president. In 1906, Ben R. Litfin, with an extensive background in the newspaper business, moved to The Dalles to work for *The Dalles Chronicle*. In 1907, he became plant foreman and two years later, with his partner, H.G. Miller, became part-owner of the newspaper. In 1915, he sold his interest to C. Hedges, but remained as manager until 1920. In 1920, in partnership with a Portland investor, he re-acquired ownership of the *Chronicle* and, three years later, bought his silent partner's interest. Subsequently, Mr. Litfin upgraded the newspaper plant's machinery and started publication of the *Weekly Chronicle*, which gained a reputation as one of the best small town weeklies in the state. *The Dalles Chronicle*, established in 1890, continues to be an influential newspaper in the Northwest.

In 1905, J.B. Kirk, an expert mechanic and machinist, opened The Dalles Iron Works, which specialized in tractors, but also handled iron and machine work. His firm manufactured the Kimball cultivator, used extensively by farmers in the Northwest. In 1907, he opened the first garage in The Dalles, but his interest centered on his machine shop. He took an active interest in civic affairs and served many years on a local school board. In 1899, Mr. Kirk married Lillie H. Johnson. Two of the couple's sons, William and Elbert, assisted their father in the operation of the shop. The Dalles Iron Works continues business in the city at a location on East Second Street. In 1907, Carlton L. Pepper entered into a partnership with S.W. Stark to establish a law practice in The Dalles. He became city attorney, serving two years, 1914-1915. In 1917, he organized The Dalles National Farm Loan Association. In addition to his business interests, he served in many capacities for civic organizations working for the betterment of the community, including the Chamber of Commerce and various fraternal organizations.

Frank G. Dick never knew his father, and his mother died when he was six years of age. He attended public schools in Iowa and, in 1908, came to The Dalles to study under Reverend G.S. Clevinger, a former teacher at Princeton University. George Blakely hired the young lad to clerk in his drug store half days while he studied law in the offices of Judge Bennett and N.J. Sinnott. After being admitted to the bar, Dick became renowned for his work in criminal law. He established his law office in the Vogt building and built an extensive and lucrative practice. Dick started investing in Wasco County land and acquired approximately 1,700 acres on which he grew wheat.

Ranching supplanted mining as the economic base of Wasco County, particularly after the railroad came through in 1882. In 1881, F.C. Clausen filed on a homestead on the Deschutes River and also secured a timber claim. Gradually, he accumulated more land until he owned about 3,000 acres. In 1882, he experimented by planting wheat, becoming a pioneer grower of that crop in Wasco County. Thomas Brogan, born in Ireland, worked as a coal miner in Pennsylvania, mined gold in New Zealand and participated in the sheep and cattle business in Australia before returning to the United States in 1892. He purchased a ranch in Wasco County and eventually accumulated 16,000 acres, becoming the largest individual Wasco County landowner at the time. He ran four thousand sheep as well as a cattle herd. He became the largest stockholder of the Citizens National Bank of The Dalles. In 1898, Delaney P. Ketchum, a dealer in livestock, principally sheep, purchased a 4,000-acre ranch east of The Dalles, where he planted about 1,000 acres of wheat with the balance in pasture. Eventually, he owned 5,000 acres along the Deschutes River and a 3,000-acre stock ranch southwest of The Dalles.

Though the new highway provided a transportation route for an increasing number of automobiles, horseback riders continued to use McUllah's livery to stable their horses. Orchardists sold fruit to Libby McNeil and Libby for canning. Flinn's Hotel featured family style dinners. The lattice work above the benches at the Chamber of Commerce building supported honeysuckle vines that attracted humming birds. And natives lived in their homes in the Lone Pine Village, just east of town.

Construction of the Twin Tunnels

Construction detail, the (unlined) Twin Tunnels (near Mosier) with the arch-rail lined view-point visible in the photograph (right).

The Columbia River Gorge from the Twin Tunnels

View of the Columbia River to the west from the Twin Tunnels observation deck.

OHC photos courtesy of Dennis Wiancko.

Twin Tunnels and Viewpoint, CRH

West Portal, Twin Tunnels, between Hood River and Mosier.

Twin Tunnels, Near Mosier

The Twin Tunnels, near Mosier, built in 1921, were recently re-opened for bicycle and foot traffic.   *Photos courtesy of George Perry VI.*

Mosier Creek Bridge

In 1920, the contracting firm, Lindstrom & Feigenson, completed this 182-foot arch bridge across Mosier Creek. Engineer Conde B. McCullough, Oregon Highway Commission, designed the structure.   *ODOT photo courtesy of Jeanette Kloos.*

The CRH East of Mosier

The unpaved highway out of Mosier passed through Mark Mayer's orchards, shown in this historic (1920) photo.   *Photo postcard courtesy of Steve Lehl.*

Dry Canyon Creek Bridge, Rowena Plateau

Dry Canyon Creek Bridge, 1921 (designed by Conde B. McCullough).

Photo courtesy of George Perry VI.

The Famous 'Mule Shoe,' Rowena Loops

The "Mule Shoe," Rowena Loops, paved in 1921.

The author's postcard collection, B.C. Markham photo.

Rowena Plateau and the Loops

The CRH descends from the Rowena Plateau to river level, then follows the river into The Dalles. *The author's postcard collection, B.C. Markham photo.*

Middle River Sternwheeler

Oregon Railroad and Navigation Company operated sternwheelers in the "middle" river between the Cascade Rapids and The Dalles until the completion of the Cascade locks in 1896. *Photo postcard, the author's collection.*

Fort Dalles

Fort Dalles became a haven for settlers during the Cayuse Indian War. The Civil War depleted the garrison, and it was abandoned in 1867.

Residential Area, The Dalles

An early, undated photograph of a residential area of The Dalles, looking north toward the Columbia River.

Photos courtesy of Steve Lehl.

Above, an early (late teens?) photograph of The Dalles, showing the CRH through town. The Narrows is visible in the upper left corner. Les dalles (literally flat stones) is the name given to a 12-mile stretch of the Columbia River below Celilo Falls, where the river has cut through lava strata forming the numerous channels of the Narrows. Below, The Dalles business district. Among the business establishments shown are the Walther-Williams Garage, that sold Dodge vehicles, A Franklin auto dealer, the Welcome Restaurant, a shoe shop, the Western Union telegraph office, the Johnson and Willerton tire shop, a grocery and another garage (looking east on Second Street). Top photo courtesy of Steve Lehl; bottom photo, David Sell.

The Dalles Business District

A view of downtown The Dalles from the promontory above E. 2nd Street, looking west. Notice the prominent building in the foreground is also visible in the photograph below.

Photo postcard, the author's collection.

Columbia River Highway, The Dalles

East Second Street (Columbia River Highway), The Dalles, looking west.

C.S. Reeves photo postcard courtesy of Steve Lehl.

214

The Dalles

Wasco County Courthouse, about 1939

United States Post Office and Hotel Dalles

O W R & N Station

Historic City Hall, The Dalles

City Hall, The Dalles, located at Fifth and Washington Streets.

Photo postcards courtesy of Steve Lehl.

Train Station, The Dalles

The Oregon-Washington Railroad and Navigation Company station served passenger and freight traffic in and out of The Dalles.

CRH, The Dalles, Oregon

Columbia River Highway, The Dalles, Oregon, early '30s. The large structure in the lower right corner of the photograph is the landmark Wasco County Flour Mill that produced White River Flour.

The Dalles Ferry

Ferry service from The Dalles to Rockland (Dallesport) commenced in 1874. In 1879, the owners, Peter Nelson and Charlie Brune, purchased the Western Queen, *a 72-foot side-wheeler. Between 1914 and 1920, the ferry was operated by W.P. Reed and Fred Smith. The latter sold it to Charlie T. Smith, who operated the ferry until the bridge was completed in 1953.*

Photo postcards courtesy of Steve Lehl.

"Les Dalles"

The Columbia River cut channels through layers of basalt, forming narrow channels. The platform in the foreground provided a place for native fishermen to net or hook a salmon.

Photo postcard courtesy of Steve Lehl.

The Narrows

Another view of "Les Dalles" upriver from the point above. The O W R & N. Company railroad line paralleled the river through the Narrows section.

Seufert Brothers Cannery

Frank and Theodore Seufert purchased a cannery at this location in 1884, which they rebuilt in 1886. Their cannery became a major factor in the canning of salmon and fruit along the Columbia River. By 1896, the plant produced 1,500 cases of canned products daily.

Photo postcards courtesy of Steve Lehl.

Celilo Falls Navigation Lock

The approximate eight-mile navigation lock (left foreground) that took river traffic around the Narrows and Celilo Falls was completed in 1915. The CRH is visible in the right foreground.

Celilo Canal, South Shore

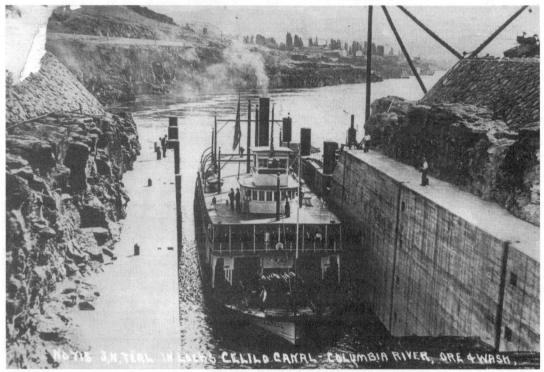

Celilo Falls marked the upriver boundary of the "Middle River," where, until the completion of the locks, a lengthy portage was required for steamship cargoes.

The CRH Bridge at Five-Mile Creek

Completion of this bridge and a 12.5-mile section of the highway east of The Dalles opened the Columbia River Highway from Pendleton to Astoria. Conde B. McCullough designed the bridge.

Native Fishery at Celilo Falls

Celilo Falls was a historic fishing and trading site for native tribes, near and far. The famous landmark and fishing ground for is now covered by the reservoir behind The Dalles dam.

Photo postcards courtesy of Steve Lehl.

The Spectacular Falls at Celilo

Celilo Falls, once a gathering place for native American tribes to fish and trade, has been stilled by the reservoir backed up by The Dalles Dam.   *Photo courtesy of George Perry VI.*

Celilo Falls, Columbia River

Native American fishery, Celilo Falls, 1930s.   *Photo courtesy of Laurel Macdonald.*

222

A view of the Columbia River and the Washington shoreline from the CRH near Celilo.
B.C. Markham photo postcard courtesy of Steve Lehl.

The CRH East of Celilo Falls

Construction detail, the graded, unpaved highway near Cape Horn (above Celilo).
Photo courtesy of George Perry VI.

The Oregon Trunk Railway Line Across The Columbia, 1912

Above, the Oregon Trunk railway line, meant to provide a route into California via the Deschutes River for the Great Northern/Northern Pacific combine, crossed the Columbia River above Celilo Falls. Note the Celilo Canal in the foreground. Below: When the Columbia River Highway came through, engineers had to build this overpass to take the highway around the obstacle presented by the line. The railway bridge opened January 7, 1912. The Oregon Trunk and the Union Pacific engaged in a battle to be the first to complete a rail line to Bend, Oregon.

Archival photos courtesy of ODOT.

Oregon Steam Navigation Company Portage Railroad, Celilo Falls

Completed in 1863, the portage railroad operated until 1882, when the railroad came through. Cape Horn is in the background; the train approaches the Deschutes River.

Photo, Corps of Engineers.

CRH Bridge, Mouth of the Deschutes River

Five-hundred nine-foot, steel-girder bridge over the Deschutes River (1919). The bridge eliminated a toll crossing in use since 1867.

Oregon Highway Commission photos courtesy of Dennis Wiancko.

Governor Zenas F. Moody's Ranch on the Deschutes River

From left, Joseph Ben (ranch employee), Dominick A., Loren and Eble Anthony, Emily Redshaw, James and Elizabeth Anthony.   *Photo courtesy of Bill Anthony.*

The Moody Ranch's Irrigation Wheel, Deschutes River

The irrigation water wheel on the east bank of the Deschutes River, which Dominick Anthony worked to install when injured (p. 198). From left), Bill, Susie and Delmer Anthony inspect the waterwheel structure where Bill's great-grandfather Dominick Anthony was injured. The shaft for the wheel is shown on the right.   *Photos courtesy of Bill Anthony.*

Sherman, Gilliam and Morrow Counties

The **Columbia River Highway** along the Columbia River across the northern boundary of **Sherman County** stretched from the Deschutes River Bridge in the west to the John Day River Bridge in the east, an approximate 15-mile section. In 1919, a contract for grading this section was let, which included the construction of five concrete bridges. A bridge about one-mile east of Biggs had to cross the O W R & N. tracks and connect with the Wasco Road up Spanish Gulch. This necessitated a bridge with approaches of 320 lineal feet and a 56-foot deck truss for the span. This section across Sherman County opened to traffic in 1920. Drifting sand created quite a problem in the county, which required oiling to prevent the build up of sand on the highway (see photograph, page 240).

Completion of the O R & N railroad in 1883 gave impetus to a change in agricultural practices in Sherman County from cattle and sheep raising to growing wheat. The O R & N stations at Biggs and Rufus became shipping points for county wheat growers, who, by 1885, produced more than 1.6 million bushels of wheat. Completion of the Columbia and Southern Railroad from Biggs to Shaniko further encouraged wheat production in the more southern reaches of the County. In Moro, Oregon, the North Pacific Flouring Mill commenced operation and shipped flour to such distant markets as China. The branch line to Shaniko survived until the Hill/Harriman combine completed a branch line to Bend.

The Stone Watchman (Near Rufus)

C 13259 - The Stone Watchman, Fleck's Orchard Blue Grass Auto Park, Half-way Between Portland & Pendleton, Oregon Trail Highways, Oregon.

The story of Henry Schadewitz is probably typical for early settlers. In 1884, Schadewitz, son of C.H. Schadewitz, a skilled wagon maker and early settler in Sherman County, preempted a homestead south of Grass Valley, where the community of Kent now stands. He cultivated some of the land and worked as a carpenter, building homes and barns for other settlers in the area. In the late 1880s, after the railroad came through, he began raising wheat in addition to hay. He added to his holdings, so that by 1900, he owned 2,000 acres, much of which he planted to wheat. In 1892, Henry Schadewitz married Emma May Parks and the couple had seven children. In 1901, he opened a general store in Kent, leasing the ranch to his sons. He owned and operated the store for five years. In 1919, he retired to a home in The Dalles.

In 1920, **Gilliam County**, except for railroad transportation, was in an isolated position because of a lack of roads. The county was in no position, economically, to pay for an extensive road system. Through state and federal funding, the Columbia River

227

Highway, routed along the Columbia River, transversed the northern border of the county. In 1919, a contract for grading the John Day River - Blalock section was awarded, which included the construction of three concrete bridges. In 1920, a contract for surfacing this approximate 15-mile section was awarded, with the work to be completed in 1921. Also in 1920, a contract for surfacing the Blalock - Arlington section of the highway was awarded, with work also to be completed in 1921. The final section of the Columbia River Highway in Gilliam County, 12.3 miles from Arlington to the Morrow County line, was located, graded and graveled by 1920. Consequently in 1921, Gilliam County had a road connecting it to The Dalles and Portland, as well as to Umatilla and Pendleton.

Prior to the coming of the railroad, the mouth of Alkali Canyon had been a shipping point for settlers' cattle and wool; the livestock fed on the lush bunch grass found in the area. In 1880, Elijah Rhea located in Alkali and built a hotel and lodging house. The first store in the town was built by Edwin B. Comfort and Thomas L. Bradbury. In 1881, James W. Smith re-located to Alkali and hired a surveyor to plat the town. He established a store with merchandise that he moved from his store on Willow Creek to the east. When the town was platted, it had three residences and the two stores. Henry Heppner built the town's third store that same year. In 1882, John Wood moved to Alkali, went into the contracting business and built many structures in the town. That same year, Leroy Weaver started a ferry service across the Columbia River to Washington. Also in 1882, August Smythe purchased a wheat and sheep ranch near Bickleton, Washington. He obtained his supplies at and marketed his wheat and wool through Arlington. After his son, Augustus K. graduated from Whitman College, father and son formed a partnership, purchased land in Gilliam County and stocked the ranch with sheep. When August Smythe died, another son, Daniel, by then a lawyer, took his father's place in the enterprise, which became the Smythe Brothers' ranches. The brothers' enterprise became one of the largest sheep operations in the western United States, with ranches in Washington, Gilliam County and Umatilla County. Augustus K. Smythe resided in Arlington, where he directed the firms operations; Dan Smythe resided in Pendleton, where he represented the partners' business interests.

By 1883, when the O R and N Company came through, the town had a blacksmith, David Mason's drug store, a hardware store, 2 hotels, 2 implement stores, a meat store, 4 mercantile stores, a wagon shop, a millinery shop, a tin shop, a harness maker, 3 saloons, 2 livery stables and a school. Other early settlers included E.B. Frum, George Leghorn and George W. Biggs. Z.F. Moody, who had business interests in several locations, built a warehouse in Arlington in the 1880s. In 1885, the legislature carved Gilliam County (which included what is now Wheeler County) from Wasco County. That year, the town of Alkali became Arlington when the Oregon Legislature granted the town a charter. The town took its new name from attorney Homer A. Comfort, whose middle name was Arlington. In the 1890s, C.C. Clark, with his wife, Nancy A. (Lambert), moved to Arlington. He purchased a general store, formerly owned by Lord and Company, and a meat market. Clark, a direct descendant of William Clark of the Lewis and Clark Expedition, served as mayor of Arlington, 1913-1918, as a county commissioner and two terms in the Oregon Legislature. During his tenure as mayor, Arlington gained a new water system, an upgraded electrical system, sidewalks and other improvements. Clark and Dr. J.W. Donnelly became part of the "good roads" movement that led to the completion of the CRH, which commenced construction in Gilliam County in 1919 and reached Arlington by 1921.

Among Arlington's native sons are Earl Snell and Carl "Doc" Severinsen. Certainly Earl W. Snell, born 1895 near Arlington of William and Nattie (Balding) Snell, gained recognition for his achievements. When his father died, Earl was sixteen. He took a job in a local garage to help support his family. Later, he and David L. Lemon became partners in the Snell and Lemon Garage in Arlington. During World War I, Snell served in the U.S. Army where his marksmanship with a rifle served him well. Snell's neighbors elected him to Arlington's city council where he served three years. In 1926, he was elected to the Oregon Legislature and served four terms, which included a term as Speaker of the House. He was then elected Secretary of State and served 8 years in that office. In 1942, Oregon voters elected Earl Snell as governor. He was re-elected in 1946. On October 28, 1947, Governor Snell was killed in an airplane crash on a goose hunting trip to Eastern Oregon.

A second noted "son" is Carl H. Severinsen, born July 7, 1927. In 1925, his father, Carl Severinsen, a dentist, started a practice in Umatilla, Oregon, but soon moved to Arlington. He married Minnie Sickle and the couple's son was born about a year later. In 1934, Carl Sr., "Big Doc," bought his son, "Little Doc," a trumpet and helped him learn to play. Soon "Little Doc" Severinsen was winning state contests as a trumpet player and was playing at ball games, banquets, luncheons, programs and recitals. In 1944, "Little Doc" formed a band, the Blue Notes. In 1949, after a stint in the Army (where he played in the band), Severinsen became a staff musician with the National Broadcasting Company. Later, he became famous as the musical director for Johnny Carson's *Tonight Show* as "Doc" Severinsen.

Condon: In 1889, Simon B. Barker located in Condon and became associated in the retail trade. He gradually increased his inventory of goods and soon owned the largest store in town. He became involved with the Oregon Life Insurance Company, which named him secretary, treasurer and a director. He founded Condon's First National Bank, engaged in ranching, accumulating several ranches, and became the largest taxpayer in Gilliam County. He married Anna Clark and the couple had five children. Another settler, Walter A. Campbell, represented the Penn Mutual Life Insurance Company in Condon many years. A native of Canada, he trained as a teacher before deciding to embark upon a career in business. He became a very successful in the life insurance business and invested his savings in land. Eventually, he accumulated more than 1,200 acres of land, which he planted principally to wheat. In 1913, voters of Wheeler, Gilliam and Sherman counties elected Campbell to the Oregon Legislature.

In June, 1919, **Morrow County** voters approved a $285,000 measure (a remarkable commitment!) for construction of "permanent" highways. Soon thereafter, construction of the 30.2-mile segment of the Columbia River Highway across Morrow County commenced. The 20.8-mile section from Castle Rock to the Umatilla County line paralleling the O W R & N. Company's tracks and the Columbia River was graded and surfaced by March, 1920. The 9.4-mile section from Castle Rock to the Gilliam County line was delayed because of an Oregon Legislative provision requiring the use of veterans of World War I in the work. Only seven veterans responded and three of those soon quit. Consequently, the original bidder was asked to complete the work on a cost-plus basis and construction proceeded. Grading and surfacing of the section was completed in October, 1919. The Coyote Cut-off necessitated a 250-foot trestle to span the O W R & N. rail line.

Jackson L. Morrow came across the plains to Oregon in 1853. He served as a lieutenant in the Indian war of 1855-56. In 1872, he moved his family to what is now Morrow County, opening a store at Stanbury's Flat in partnership with Henry Heppner. In 1885, Morrow was elected to the Oregon Legislature, where he took an active role in separating Morrow County from Wasco County, with Heppner named as the temporary county seat. The citizens of Heppner subscribed to a bond issue and built the court house at Heppner, which was dedicated on July 4, 1885. This action secured the county seat for the town. Heppner became an incorporated town in 1887, with Henry Blackman elected as its first mayor. In 1889, its citizens secured the right of way and donated land for a depot, thus securing a branch line of the O R & N Company from Willow. That year, Morrow, Tom Quaid, Lum Rhea, Henry Blackman and J.B. Natter formed a company and built the Palace Hotel. Jackson Morrow married Nancy McEwen. Their son,

J.W. Morrow, served a county clerk of Morrow County and represented Morrow, Grant and Harney counties as a state senator. He also started the first newspaper in Morrow County. Later, he went to work for the Union Pacific Railroad.

A native of Scotland, Robert F. Hynd, who spent several years as a sailor, decided to settle in Oregon and obtained employment on a river boat on the Willamette River. In Portland, he attended a play that asked the question, "What are you doing with your life?" Hynd recalled that question caused him to think seriously about his future and he decided to make better use of his talents. He left Portland and obtained work near Heppner. He learned agriculture by working on various ranches and saved most of his wages. In 1889, he embarked on his plan, purchasing a small band of sheep. A year later, he formed a partnership with W.B. Barrett in the sheep business. In 1893, he located in Heppner, becoming manager of the Morrow County Warehouse Company. Shortly thereafter he formed the Heppner Milling Company, which he managed and expanded, shipping most of its output to the far east. He also organized the Penland Livestock Company, becoming secretary/treasurer, which also expanded under his leadership to own 35,000 thousand acres of land on which the company ran 25,000 sheep. The latter business was sold to the Minor brothers near the turn of the century. Hynd continued as manager of the Heppner Warehouse and Milling Company, which shipped between three and four million pounds of wool to market from Heppner. Hynd also organized the Farmers Elevator Company and worked to expand its scope and activities. His suffered a great personal loss from the flood of 1903, which took the life of his wife, Zoe (Sigsbee) Hynd and the couple's two children. He recovered from his business losses, but withdrew from active management in 1911, and retired to Portland. He passed away on May 26, 1921, age 54.

Lewis and Clark: The expedition used canoes in descending the Columbia River in October and November, 1805. On their return up the river in 1806, the party abandoned their canoes below the narrows and obtained horses to continue their trek upriver. On April 27, 1806, the explorers, on the north bank, passed the mouth of the Umatilla River and proceeded another 9 miles and encamped. Chief Yellept of the "Wollawollahs" [Walla Wallas], whom the explorers had dealt with on the journey westward, invited the expedition members to "remain at his village for three or four days, during which he would supply us with the only food they had, and furnish us with horses for our journey." Yellept also presented "a fine white horse" to Captain Clark. A grateful Clark presented the Chief with his sword, ammunition and powder and other small gifts. Because of the friendship of Chief Yellept and his tribe, the expedition could continue on their overland homeward journey much better prepared for the rigors that awaited them.

Of interest are the estimates by Captain Lewis and Captain Clark concerning the native population they found living along the Columbia River in 1805-1806. From what is now Astoria to the "Multnomah [Willamette] River," their recorded estimate of the population was 19,000 "souls;" from the Willamette to the "Wallawollah [Walla Walla] River, 14,440 "souls." Fred Lockley, "First Names," *Conversations with Pioneer Men,* Rainy Day Press, Eugene, Oregon, page 319. According to Robert Boyd, *People of The Dalles, The Indians of Wascopam Mission,* University of Nebraska Press, Lincoln, 1996, Lewis and Clark's native population estimate, the Cascades to the Snake River, was 10,400. Experts agree that introduced contagious diseases had decimated the native population. Two smallpox epidemics prior to the expedition's descent of the Columbia River in 1805 took an estimated 30-40% of the population. In the 1830s, mortality from a "fever [malaria] and ague" epidemic was heavy. Whooping cough, dysentery and finally, measles, took many native lives. The latter probably led to the Whitman Massacre and the start of the Cayuse War.

A Wool "Train"

Flocks of sheep contributed to the early prosperity of Wasco (later, Sherman) County. Wagon trains transported wool from Shaniko to The Dalles and from other scouring mills to Pendleton.

Photo courtesy of George Perry VI.

Biggs - Maryhill Ferry

In 1915, piqued because a ferry operator kept him waiting, Sam Hill established a ferry service with his Governor West from his Maryhill Estate to Biggs Junction. Soon, however, his poorly designed craft failed. J.H. Robinson also operated a ferry service at this locale.

Photo postcards courtesy of Steve Lehl.

Oregon-Washington Railroad Station, Biggs, Oregon

Served by the railroad and steamboats, the new Columbia River Highway provided an alternative, competitive means for Eastern Oregon ranchers to transport their products to market. *Photo courtesy of Dave Wand.*

Fleck's Auto Camp

Fleck's Auto Camp, almost mid-way between the Dalles and Arlington, was located beneath the stone Watchman (near the town of Rufus, Oregon).

Rufus, Oregon

Entrepeneurs quickly established tourist facilities along the new CRH, which brought travelers to this formerly somewhat isolated part of the state. Photo courtesy of Steve Lehl.

Huck Home, Rufus

Bill and Bessie Huck moved from Twin Bridges (mouth of the John Day River) to this home in Rufus. Visiting Bessie Huck is a former neighbor, Emma (Lampert) Fox, of Early, Oregon.
Bessie Huck photo collection, courtesy of Dave Wand.

The John Day Dam

With the completion of the dams on the Columbia, culminating with the completion of John Day Dam in 1964, the character of the great river changed from its raw, turbulent and churning past to a series of placid impoundments that would astound Lewis and Clark and early motorists who traveled the CRH.   *Photo, the author.*

George Fox, Mouth of the John Day River

George Fox takes a moment to enjoy the view from this sand flat near the Columbia River at the mouth of the John Day River.   *Photo courtesy of Dave Wand.*

234

Wheat Harvest, Ranches, Near Early, Oregon

Above: A horse-drawn combine harvests wheat on a ranch near Early, Oregon, close to the mouth of the John Day River. Below: A steam-driven tractor powers a threshing machine to thrash wheat. The thresher crew, from left: Fat Walker, Wallace Fields, Dan McDermitt, Howard Boals, Charles Hull, Cleland May, Charles Adams, Earl Bowlby, Bill Williams, Frank Hull, unknown, unknown, unknown, Ivan Clark and Charley Warren.

Bessie Huck photo collection, courtesy of Dave Wand.

235

Wheat Harvest Near Early, OR. Columbia River Sternwheeler

Left: The threshing crew takes a break from work, which involved laboring in the hot, dusty, dry and chaff-filled air around the threshing machine. Right: Ranchers took sacked wheat to the wharf by wagon, then loaded it aboard a sternwheeler bound for The Dalles.

Bessie Huck photo collection, courtesy of Dave Wand.

Early, Oregon, Residents Host Visitors ca 1921

The Fox family, residents of Early, Oregon, take a relative from Troutdale, Oregon, on a tour of the highway near the mouth of the John Day River. From left, Rose Fox, Jim Fox, Alex Lampert and Emma (Lampert) Fox (wife of Jim Fox). A second visitor, John Seidl, also of Troutdale, took the photo.

Photo courtesy of Dave Wand.

236

Construction of the Highway Bridge, John Day River

Construction crews bridge the John Day River near its mouth, just upstream from the O-W R & N. Bridge. Bill Huck is credited with giving the locale the name, Twin Bridges. Below, left: Looking east toward the bridge. Below right, looking north toward the mouth of the John Day and the Columbia River.   *Bessie Huck photo collection, courtesy of Dave Wand.*

"Twin Bridges," John Day River

The railroad and highway bridges cross the John Day River near its mouth. The garage, right foreground, was owned and operated by Bill Huck. The garage, store and camp across the highway were owned by Herbert K. Porter.   *Bessie Huck photo collection, courtesy of Dave Wand.*

Porter's Business Complex

Another view of Herbert K. Porter's business establishments at the east end of the highway bridge across the John Day River.   *Photo collection, Bessie Huck, courtesy of Dave Wand.*

Huck Station and Home, Twin Bridges

Bob Huck, with his wife Bessie, built a garage and a home at the east end of the John Day Bridge shortly after its completion. They lived here until the highway was "slightly repositioned," which caused them to move to Rufus (see p. 233).

Photo collection, Bessie Huck, courtesy of Dave Wand.

Highway Traveler, 1919

Not yet finished, the highway attracted this traveler.   Photo courtesy of Dave Wand.

Diversion Dam, John Day River, Early, Oregon ca 1921

Water from the John Day River powered a grist mill at Early, which produced flour for the area's residents. From left, the individuals are: John Seidl, visitor from Troutdale, Emma Fox, Rose Fox (sister of Jim Fox) and Alex Lampert, a second visitor from Troutdale. The Troutdale visitors traveled the newly opened Columbia River Highway to reach Early.

Photo collection, Bessie Huck, courtesy of Dave Wand.

Highway Construction in Gilliam County

Oiling sand dunes in Gilliam County to stabilize blowing sand that drifted over the new CRH.
OHC photo courtesy of Dennis Wiancko.

Arlington, Oregon

The CRH in the foreground and the tracks of the Union Pacific along the Columbia River, provide transportation links for the town of Arlington. Arlington, located at the mouth of Alkali Canyon, originally was known as Alkali. Photo postcard courtesy of Steve Lehl.

Arlington Shell Station

Bill Head's Arlington service station provided gasoline and other services for travelers on the CRH in the eastern part of the State. Photo courtesy of Steve Lehl.

Business District, Arlington

The Arlington Bakery (left) featured "lunches, candies and home made ice cream." Across the street, the Arlington Hotel (formerly the McFadden), a drug store, a confectionary and a garage are visible.   *B.C. Markham photo courtesy of Steve Lehl.*

Arlington's Grain Elevators

Cargill's grain elevator along the Columbia River provided a distinctive landmark for the City of Arlington.   *Photo postcard courtesy of Steve Lehl.*

Willow Creek Bridge, Gilliam County

The concrete span over Willow Creek near Heppner Junction in Gilliam County.

OHC photo courtesy of Dennis Wiancko.

Mouth of the Umatilla River

The Union Pacific Railroad bridge crosses the Umatilla River near its mouth. The railroad had a major facility at Umatilla, including a roundhouse.   *Photo courtesy of Steve Lehl.*

McNary Dam, 1955

From tidewater, dams along the Columbia River Highway to Umatilla include: Bonneville, The Dalles, John Day and McNary. The dams, built from 1933 to 1964, completely altered the appearance and character of the Columbia River. The two major river obstructions to navigation, the Cascade Rapids and Celilo Falls, were inundated behind Bonneville Dam and The Dalles Dam, respectively

The CRH , Eastern Oregon

After following the Columbia River for some 300 miles, at Umatilla the highway turned southeastward to reach Hermiston, Stanfield, Echo, Reith and Pendleton.

Photo postcards courtesy of Steve Lehl.

Umatilla County - Umatilla, Hermiston, Stanfield and Echo

The Oregon Highway Commission awarded the contract for grading and graveling the Columbia River Highway from the Morrow County line via Umatilla, Hermiston and Stanfield to Echo in 1919. The highway paralleled the O W R & N. Company tracks and the Columbia River to the Umatilla River, and crossed the Umatilla near Hermiston. The work was completed in 1920. In the biennium, 1923-24, construction of a new bridge across the Umatilla River provided access via the CRH into Umatilla. During the 1925-26 biennium, most sections of the CRH east of The Dalles were oiled with hot tar, then covered with gravel, including (presumably) the Umatilla County section. This provided a paved surface called oiled macadam. By 1928, according to the 8th biennial highway commission report, the CRH from Astoria to Pendleton had been paved, either with a bituminous mixture (Warrenite) or oiled macadam.

Umatilla: The frontier town of Umatilla, at the confluence of the Umatilla River with the Columbia, was platted in 1863. The first town in Umatilla County, it served as the county seat from 1865 to 1869. Originally called Umatilla Landing, it became an important shipping point during gold rush days when stagecoaches, pack trains and freight wagons plied the wagon roads between Umatilla Landing and the John Day mines, Auburn and Boise City. From Umatilla, the Oregon Steam Navigation Company's sternwheelers took gold and other goods down the Columbia to Portland, where the gold was shipped on to San Francisco. Homesteaders took up claims and by the 1870s, wheat and wool had replaced gold as the principal products shipped down river. The trip from Umatilla to Portland took two days and included a portage of approximately 15 miles to pass Celilo Falls and The Narrows and a six-mile portage at the Cascade Rapids. The town had several saloons, three hotels, mercantile stores, a meat market and storage facilities for hay, grain, feed and seed. In 1879, Jehu Switzler commenced operating a horse-powered ferry that crossed the Columbia River at Umatilla. By 1883, Henry Villard's O R & N had completed a railroad line from Wallula to Portland. A line to Pendleton was in use by 1882 and the Company had a roundhouse at Umatilla. A Umatilla historian remarked that Umatilla Landing merchants made fortunes during the landing's boom times, then "took their money to Pendleton." Certainly, one early Umatilla Landing merchant, Lot Livermore, moved to Pendleton in 1866, opened a general store, became Pendleton's postmaster and, in 1880, was elected as Pendleton's first mayor. Despite the "relocations," Umatilla's population nearly doubled between 1910 and 1920, from 198 to 390 individuals. In 1921, Umatilla's mayor was M.F. Davis, and Mark A. Cleveland edited both the *Umatilla Spokesman* and the *Stanfield Standard*.

Hermiston: The Federal Reclamation Act of 1902 followed by Oregon's Irrigation Act of 1905 gave impetus to the construction of the Umatilla Project, 1906 - 1908. A diversion dam across the Umatilla River diverted water through a concrete pipeline to Cold Springs Dam to form the Cold Springs Reservoir. The project, a monumental effort, provided irrigation water for settlers who had taken up land claims in the area. With irrigation came water-dependent crops such as alfalfa, corn, melons, potatoes, sugar beets, hops, mint, fruit orchards (which, unfortunately, proved unsuitable) and crops needed for dairy cattle, hogs and poultry, which provided an alternative to wheat and stock raising. Irrigation changed the character of the land surrounding what is now Hermiston from sand and sagebrush to farm land. Two firms, the Maxwell Company and Newport and Skinner, competed to build the town of Hermiston, which was incorporated in 1907. At that time, the *Hermiston Herald* proudly reported that 100 new homes were nearing completion adding to the 4 situated there just five months earlier. By 1910, Hermiston's population had grown to 647; in the next decade it increased by 9 to 656 people. In 1907, Frank B. Swayze opened the First Bank of Hermiston. In 1909, his bank absorbed the Hermiston Bank and Trust Company and became the First National Bank of Hermiston. Swayze moved to a large building made of stone located on First and Main.

The town's name, Hermiston, came from Robert Louis Stevenson's novel, *The Weir of Hermiston*. It was suggested by Mrs. Joseph F. McNaught, wife of Hermiston's first postmaster. (Though a minister, Reverend E.R. Hermiston, came to Hermiston in 1907 with his private railroad car, "Emmanuel," and established the First Baptist Church, as the *Hermiston Herald* explained, the town was not named for the reverend.) By 1912, Hermiston had two hotels, the Hermiston and the Hotel Oregon, the First Bank of Hermiston, a depot on the O W R & N. Company line, Oron O. Felthouse's sand, gravel, ice and transportation businesses, Oregon Hardware and other commercial establishments. Hermiston's two-story, stone school housed both elementary and high school students. In addition to the aforementioned Baptist church, a Methodist Church and the 'Our Lady of the Angels' Catholic Church (1922) served local congregations. In 1921, F.C. McKenzie served as Mayor of Hermiston; Bernard Mainwaring edited the *Hermiston Herald*.

Erma Ostrom, Umatilla

Erma Ostrom, Glenn Ostrom Texaco on the Columbia River Highway, Umatilla. **Photo** *courtesy of the Umatilla (City) Historical Museum.*

Stanfield: After graduating from Eastern Oregon Normal School, Robert N. Stanfield assumed management of his father's sheep ranch. By 1920, Stanfield had 350,000 sheep and owned approximately three million acres of ranchland. Later, Robert N. Stanfield became a United States Senator. In 1904, he purchased (for $8700) what was to become the site of Stanfield. Subsequently, Dr. Henry W. Coe purchased the property and platted the townsite, naming it after the prior owner. W. J. Furnish, former sheriff of Umatilla County and mayor of Pendleton, established the Inland Irrigation and Furnish Ditch Companies. Previously, he had engaged in the wool commission business and had also acquired an interest in the Pendleton Savings Bank. The two companies (Inland and Furnish) constructed the Furnish-Coe dam on the Umatilla River to bring irrigation water to more than 10,000 acres in the area. Dr. Coe formed the Columbia Land Company, and sold, as an agent for Furnish, land to be served by the system. The developers promoted the planting of orchards, but the area's cold spring weather hampered pollination. Later, silting and other problems caused the project to be taken over by the U.S.

Reclamation Service. Because of these difficulties, Stanfield's population actually declined from 318 in 1910 to 278 in 1920. Located on the O W R & N. line, Stanfield had several commercial establishments including the Stanfield Bank, the *Stanfield Register* (later, the *Stanfield Standard*), the Inland Empire Lumber Company, the Stanfield Swiss Cheese factory, the Umatilla Storage and Commission Company warehouse (with cooling rooms and cold storage plant for handling fruit, dairy and poultry products) and the Stanfield Hotel. Stanfield was the home of the Stanfield Grange, three churches (Presbyterian, Catholic and Pentecostal) and the Reeves School (made of stone). In 1923, Congress authorized the McKay Dam and Reservoir project, which, when completed in 1927, gave the irrigation district a more stable and plentiful water supply.

Echo: Echo, noted for its flour mill, was founded by James H. Koontz, who gave the town the name, Echo, to honor his daughter, Echo Koontz. Koontz established the Henrietta Flour Mill, which he named after Fort Henrietta, erected in 1855 by Oregon volunteers after an Indian uprising. Members of local tribes had burned Utilla, the first Indian Agency, which was located across the Umatilla River. By 1907, Echo boasted 45 business and professional establishments, including a wool-scouring plant, a flour mill and the Echo Hotel, the largest hotel on the O.W. R. & N. Company system. In addition to these enterprises, Echo had a general mercantile store, Jones Livery, an O W R & N. depot, the Hoskins Hotel, the *Echo News* building, the George and Miller Company store, Spinning's drug store, W.H. Boyd's store, George Pearson's Red Express and a creamery. Echo's population grew from 400 in 1910 to 501 in 1920. St. Peter's Catholic Church, erected in 1913, and the Methodist Church, established in 1886, served the Christian community. In 1921, the local newspaper, the *Echo News*, was edited by W.H. Crary.

Joseph Cunha, born in the Azore Islands, stowed away on a ship that landed in Boston. He made his way west to California, where he somehow learned that a countryman, Antone J. Vey, had a sheep ranch in Oregon. Cunha traveled to Umatilla County and landed a job with Vey. After saving his money for three years, Cunha managed to buy 1,200 old ewes, took up a land claim near Butter Creek and commenced building his flock. His sheep ranch prospered, enabling Cunha to purchase the Henrietta Flour Mill, which he renamed the Echo Flour Mill. By 1944, Joseph Cunha owned 60,000 acres of grazing land, 14,000 sheep, 600 Hereford cattle and the mill, which by that time was used as a feed mill and warehouse.

Umatilla River Bridge

Originally, the CRH crossed the Umatilla near Hermiston. After 1925, this bridge took travelers across the Umatilla River into the city of Umatilla. In 1951, the bridge was widened, at which time decorative railings were removed.
Modified photo, the author.

Umatilla Landing

The Umatilla House was one of three hotels in the frontier town of Umatilla Landing (later, Umatilla), the Orleans, the Idaho and the Umatilla House. The two other business establishments in the photograph are Cherry's Saloon and the Star Restaurant.

Photo, Matt Johnson, Howdyshell Studio, Pendleton.

Guerin's Texaco Station, Umatilla

Clarence V. Guerin's Texaco service station on the Columbia River Highway, Umatilla, early 1930s. *Photo courtesy of the Umatilla (City) Museum.*

Wheat Harvest, Pre-Combine Era

Threshing Grain

Harvesting wheat, cutting the grain with mowing machines. Next, a reaper bundled the grain in sheafs to dry before threshing took place. Notice the bundled sheafs stacked in the fields to dry.
Photo postcard, the author.

Hermiston, Oregon

The Hermiston Hotel, a cafe and drug store along the CRH in the City of Hermiston, late '30s or early '40s.
Photo postcard courtesy of Steve Lehl.

This marker in front of the Echo Historical Museum records some of the early history of the area. *Photo, the author.*

The marker reads:

Echo Historical Museum

Utilla 1851
Fort Henrietta 1855
Echo 1881

"The old Oregon Trail crossed the Umatilla River to the Indian Agency, Utilla, which was established here in 1851. When the Agency was burned by Indians in 1855, soldiers erected Fort Henrietta in its place. The cottonwood fort was later destroyed by soldiers when the Indian hostilities ceased. The present town of Echo was laid out and established in 1881 by James H. Koontz, who named the town after his small daughter [Echo]."

Echo, Oregon

A reminder of Echo's founder, James H. Koontz, is emblazoned on this historic building in Echo.   *Modified photo, the author.*

Seats of the Gods

"Seats of the Gods" near Barnhart Canyon, CRH along the Umatilla River approaching Reith.
OHC photo courtesy of Dennis Wiancko

Wheat Farming With Horses

Wheat farming with horses and mules. Upper left: Plowing wheat land with horses - the plows are likely 4-bottom. Upper right: Cutting wheat with mowing machines. Middle left: Harvesting wheat with a combine pulled by 38 horses. Middle right: Horse teams working in tandem harvest grain. Lower: Horses pull an early model combine to harvest grain. The Pendleton Iron Works manufactured combines under license. Photos courtesy of George Perry VI.

Umatilla County - Reith and Pendleton

The Oregon State Highway Commission applied to the Bureau of Public Roads to make the Echo-Pendleton section of the CRH a "post road," which would bring federal funds for the project. The contract for grading and graveling the section was let early in 1920 with a projected completion date in 1921. In 1904, to improve its streets, Pendleton had paved its principal thoroughfares, the second Oregon city to do so. According to the Oregon Highway Commission's report, by the 8th biennium (1927-28), the section of the CRH into Pendleton had been paved with hot tar and gravel.

Rieth: Rieth, near Pendleton, became one the Union Pacific Railroad's busiest switchyards. The town took its name from pioneer settlers who owned the land when, in 1916, the Union Pacific Railroad established its yard. In 1917, George Vichas built the Rieth Hotel, which housed railroad workers of the Union Pacific. After prohibition ended, he added the Silver Dollar Night Club, which became a popular dining spot. When the Union Pacific moved its division station to Hinkle in 1950, Rieth lost a significant payroll. George Vichas kept the hotel and the Silver Dollar open until he retired in 1960. Other commercial establishments included the Fletcher Oil Company, the General Gasoline establishment (where the post office was located) and Sargant and Grant's general merchandise store. Children in the area attended the Rieth School, constructed in 1910.

Reith, Oregon 1944

The Columbia River Highway winds through Reith while the Union Pacific line cuts a swath across the landscape. The meandering Umatilla River provides a backdrop for the wheat fields that cover the background hills.   *Photo, Matt Johnson, Howdyshell studio, Pendleton.*

Pendleton, Oregon

A photograph of Pendleton taken near the time when the State extended the Columbia River Highway to Pendleton.   *Photo, Matt Johnson, Howdyshell Studio.*

Pendleton: In 1862, Moses Goodwin traded Abram Miller a span of mules for a quarter-section of land along the Umatilla River. In 1865, Goodwin constructed a bridge across the river and erected a hotel (Goodwin Hotel) near the crossing. A townsite was platted in 1868 by E.A. Wilson and given the name, Pendleton, after Senator George H. Pendleton, candidate for vice-president on the Democratic ticket in 1864. (A slate of General George McClellan and Pendleton opposed President Abraham Lincoln's bid for a second term.) Three years after Umatilla County separated from Wasco County in 1862, the town of Umatilla became the county seat. In 1868, in a hotly contested election, proponents of a more centrally located county seat prevailed and, in 1869, county offices moved to the newly established town of Pendleton. Moses Goodwin donated two and one-half acres for county buildings. Pendleton received its charter in 1880 and elected city officers. Lot Livermore, merchant and postmaster, became the first mayor.

The O R & N line from Umatilla reached Pendleton in 1882. Henry Villard, financier and president of the railroad, built the three-story Villard House at Main and Court. By 1887, Pendleton had piped water as well as electricity. In 1888-89, Umatilla County built a new courthouse in the French Renaissance style with a richly ornamented roof line featuring four cupolas, one above each wing. A central clock-tower featured a large Seth-Thomas clock with four faces, which Dr. Frederick W. Vincent (dentist) had urged the county to purchase. In 1880, the city arranged to purchase 640 acres of Indian reservation lands on which to expand. In 1882, Congress approved the sale of reservation lands to allow Pendleton more room for growth. As a consequence, the approximate 292,000 acre reservation was reduced by about 140,000 acres. Public sale of the land commenced in 1891. Fires and floods caused problems for Pendleton residences and businesses. After a major flood in 1882, construction of a levee helped prevent severe flooding until 1906, when the levee gave way and flood waters from the Umatilla River inundated the town. During the 1890s, fires took many historic buildings, including the Villard Hotel, the Golden Rule Hotel, the Webfoot saloon, the Transfer House and Byers Mill. Despite these setbacks, by 1912 Pendleton had six hotels, the Bowman, the Golden Rule, the LaFontaine, the Pendleton, the St. George and the St. Elmo, which provides evidence of the resilient nature of its people and the importance of Pendleton as a regional transportation center.

Early Pendleton industries included the Pendleton Wool-Scouring and Packaging Company, incorporated in 1893, the well-known Pendleton Woolen Mills, incorporated in 1895, and the Pendleton Iron Works, 1897. The wool scouring mill, which operated for about a decade, supplied wool for the woolen mill, which started producing woolen blankets. By 1905, the interest of the mill's Eastern backers had faded and production declined. However, encouraged by Edwin Aldrich, editor of the *East Oregonian*, local leaders persuaded Clarence M. and Roy T. Bishop, sons of C.P. and Fannie Bishop, associated with a Salem woolen mill, to buy the Pendleton mill. The Bishops had learned the wool trade from their grandfather, Thomas Kay, who owned the woolen mill in Salem. In 1912, the brothers purchased a fabric mill in Washougal, Washington. In 1924, Pendleton Woolen Mills introduced patterned garments with the production of men's woolen shirts. This innovation led to a more complete line of both men and women's wear in addition to the firm's blankets, saddle blankets, yard goods and other products. Pendleton Woolen Mills is vertically integrated. The company starts with raw wool and completes every step of the manufacturing process in its own plant to produce woolen rugs, blankets and other woven products. The company also produces the fabrics used in its garments, but the finished men's and women's wear is stitched by others. Much of the wool used in the company's products comes from local sheep ranches. One wool supplier, the Cunningham family ranch, has been providing the Pendleton mill with wool for more than 70 years. The Pendleton Iron Works manufactured farm machinery and arranged with patent holders to make the first Reynolds threshers for area farmers. By 1909, Pendleton Iron Works had produced six Reynolds threshing machines, which promised an "exciting future" according to many farmers.

Wheat growing and livestock raising, particularly sheep, dominated the agricultural economy of the Pendleton area. An early settler, Green Arnold, was among the first growers to try planting wheat. John Bowman homesteaded on Birch Creek, where his son, Oliver P. Bowman grew wheat. John Bowman also established a livery and feed business across from the Pendleton Hotel on Main Street. Grain farmer W.W. Harrah introduced a new harvest method for wheat growers when he had the Penland Brothers build him wagons to hold bulk grain, which he then used with his combine to eliminate the sacking of wheat. He hauled his bulk wheat to the railhead where he put it in paper-lined box cars for shipment to Portland. In 1929, in response to plunging grain prices, local grain growers met to form the Pendleton Grain Growers (PGG). The Agricultural Marketing Act of 1929 encouraged the formation of such groups to enable "the farmer to help himself." Local growers became part of a larger organizational network, the Farmers National Grain Corporation and the North Pacific Grain Growers. These organizations helped stabilize grain prices and PGG became profitable immediately. PGG built a feed plant, owned a large, wooden, grain elevator that became a landmark in Pendleton and expanded its services to farmers. PGG has served its members well and has become a major factor in the area's economy as well as having a positive impact on Oregon's agricultural base. Umatilla County's wheat production places it among the top wheat producing counties in the United States. Wheat farming progressed from horse-drawn implements, including the first combines, to tractor-drawn machinery, then to self-propelled machines.

Sheep ranching became so common that county hillsides, according to one observer, were splotched with white. The Dalles and Pendleton both became major shipping points for wool. In the early 1890s, the two transportation hubs shipped over 10,000,000 pounds of wool. By 1900, Pendleton had become the principal wool market in the United States. In addition to Joseph Cunha, the Cunningham ranch and Robert Stanfield, each mentioned previously, other sheep ranches and ranchers included the Beauchamp ranch (Umapine), J.N. Burgess (Pilot Rock), Jacob Frazer (Birch Creek), the Mann ranch (Echo), and David Shaw (upper McKay Creek), among others.

The area's wheat production encouraged the development of the flour milling industry. In 1866, William G. Preston purchased a one-half interest in the Washington Flouring Mills, located in Waitsburg, Washington. He and his brother, Platt A. Preston, acquired control of mills in Athena, Milton-Freewater and Pendleton, which operated as the Preston Brothers mills. Eventually, the business became the Preston-Schaffer Milling Company. By 1875, wheat production had reached a significant level. That year, W.S. Byers built his first flour mill at S.E. Fifth and Court Streets. The quality of his flour was such that, in 1893, "Byers' Best" took first premium at the Columbia Exposition, Chicago World's Fair. Byers Avenue honors Byers' memory. Byers' mill burned in 1897 and was rebuilt in 1898. After Byers died, his daughter, Sophie (Byers) McComas, managed the mill until her death in 1941. She left a legacy of more than $500,000 for the care of Pendleton's elderly. The mill became the Western Milling Company, which burned in 1947. In 1887, Dr. Frederick Vincent founded the company that used the Byers' millrace to generate electricity. The company merged into Pacific Power and Light in 1910. Another flour mill, owned by Fred Walters, operated from about 1887 until it burned in 1945.

Other individuals and business establishments prospered. Sheep rancher Jacob Frazer invested in Pendleton real estate, including the First National Bank Building (1882) and the Frazer Opera House (1886). Frazer Avenue was named in his memory. C.S. 'Sam' Jackson, intrigued by the possibilities offered by the growing western town came west in 1880. He first took a job as an agent for a stage company. Taking advantage of other opportunities, he engaged in a number of profitable ventures before purchasing, with John Guyer in 1881, the *East Oregonian* from L.B. Cox. Cox had purchased the newspaper from John Bentley and J.L. Turner. After a few months, J.P. Wagner, lawyer from New York, became Jackson's partner by purchasing John Guyer's half-interest. The newspaper became a daily in 1888. Wagner withdrew from the paper in 1890, leaving Jackson its sole owner. In 1902, Jackson purchased the *Portland Evening Journal,* renaming it the *Oregon Journal.* He retained an interest in the *East Oregonian,* naming Edwin B. Aldrich editor in 1908. In 1913, he sold his interest in the paper to Aldrich.

In 1881, William "Billy" Roesch purchased the City Brewery, which produced a well-known brand, Elkhorn Beer, until prohibition stopped production. The plant then produced soft drinks until prohibition ended in 1933. Another brewery, owned by Henry Schultz, produced a popular Pilsner beer. His plant also produced ice. W.J. Lemp located his brewery and cold storage plant close to the wool scouring and packing plant. Western Union opened a telegraph office in 1883. In 1900, three brothers, A.C., Otto W. and Fred W. Koeppen, opened A.C. Koeppen & Bros., Druggists, on Court Street. It was "67 steps from Main toward the Courthouse." A.C. managed the pharmacy, where he dispensed his own formulations, including Koeppen's Medicated Foot Powder. Otto W. kept the books and Fred W. ran the soda fountain, which is remembered for its marble counter and homemade ice cream topped by freshly crushed wild huckleberries from the Blue Mountains (15 cents). In 1902, Lawrence Frazier purchased the Blue Front Stationery at 237 S. Main from Max Baer. Ben Burrough's lumber yard provided building materials during Pendleton's early years of growth. In 1905, a well-known saddle and western equipment company, Hamley & Company, opened a plant and store in Pendleton. The firm produced saddles, chaps and other western gear that found a ready market. Pendleton also boasted of "the only cigar maker in Umatilla County," the Pioneer Cigar Factory.

Pendleton's downtown district, similar in this respect to Astoria, has a labyrinth of underground passageways that stretch from S.W. Frazer Avenue to the Umatilla River (5 blocks) and one or two blocks east and west from the tunnels under Main Street. Apparently, these tunnels were used by merchants to move merchandise, money and spirits to stores, banks and saloons, respectively. According to accounts, some tunnels were used by prostitutes (and their customers) to access the "second-story establishments" in which the ladies conducted their trade. In the early 1880s Henry Villard had used Chinese laborers in the construction of the O R & N line into Pendleton. During this period, Pendleton's underground became "home" to Chinese workers. The Chinese extended and improved the tunnel system to gain access to their establishments, which could thus be reached without the necessity of using the public streets. Tours of a section of these underground passageways are conducted by Pendleton Underground Tours, 37 S.W. Emigrant Avenue. Tourists visit a century old cardroom, a "rooming house" for Chinese laborers, a Chinese laundry, a prohibition speakeasy and gambling hall, a meat market, an opium den and more. The tour includes a former second-story bordello, "Cozy Rooms," managed by Madam Stella Darby, that operated until closed in 1953.

In 1909, Pendleton citizens, in hopes of curbing "unrest." sponsored a successful 4th of July celebration. In 1910, the group organized the Northwestern Frontier Exhibition Association, elected J. Roy Raley, President, and sponsored its first rodeo. Raley's father, Colonel James H. Raley, came with his parents to Pendleton in 1864. He served in several local offices and the Oregon State Senate. In 1911, Raley resigned in favor of Sheriff Til Taylor, but continued working on behalf of the association. That same year, the association called for bids to build a grandstand. In 1914, the rodeo added the *Happy Canyon Pageant*, written by Raley, that depicted the coming of the white man. His son, with a flair for drama, produced the first full-length movie of the Pendleton Round-Up. The annual show thrived until the early thirties, when the onset of the depression caused indebtedness to grow. Lawrence Frazier, board member from 1910-1937, headed an interim board, which declared the association defunct. E.N. Boylen, in his book, *Episode of the West*, said "The Round-Up was broke but not whipped." Frazier and his interim board of directors reorganized as the Pendleton Round-Up Association. Profits from 1935 to 1938 cleared the debt and the world famous Pendleton Round-Up continues to attract thousands of people to its annual rodeo, show and exhibition. Boylen also noted, "Lol [Frazier] could get as much out of a dime for which most required a silver dollar."

Til Taylor served more than twenty years as a deputy or Sheriff of Umatilla County. In the 1870s, his father, David Taylor, of Athena, had served as a deputy under Sheriff J.L. Sperry. In 1875, an uncle, D.M. Taylor, opened a blacksmith shop in Pendleton. In 1902, voters elected Til Taylor Sheriff of Umatilla County. On July 25, 1920, six men lodged in the county jail broke out, killing Sheriff Taylor in the successful attempt. County commissioners appointed W.J. 'Jinks' Taylor as sheriff to replace his brother in the post. The killers, Emmett Brancroft alias Neil Hart, Elvie Kirby alias James Owens and John L. "Jack" Rathie, were caught, convicted and hanged. Two others involved, Elvin L. Stoop, alias Lewis Anderson, and Floyd Henderson, alias Richard Patterson, received life sentences (released in 1934 after their sentences were commuted by Governor Julius Meier). Of the sixth prisoner, Albert Lindgren, little is known, apparently because he was not directly involved in the murder. Sheriff Til Taylor is memorialized by an equestrian statue of him leading a Round-Up parade located in the Pendleton park that bears his name. In 1929, the bronze statue, designed by sculptor A. Phimister Proctor and cast in Paris, France, came via a Penland Brothers truck from Portland to Pendleton on the Columbia River Highway [Highway 30]. Because of the statue's height, Til Taylor's bronze hat had to be removed for the journey.

In 1914, the Penland brothers purchased their first truck, which was to be used to haul groceries from Walla Walla, Washington, to Pendleton. Previously, they had used horse-drawn wagons to deliver groceries and other items to Pendleton customers. After World War I, George Simpson pioneered the first truck line between Pendleton and Walla Walla. The Pendleton Auto Company sold Franklin and Reo automobiles. Ebrel & Temple sold implements, vehicles and farm supplies (1921). In 1922, Wallace Brothers' Garage sold a new Studebaker to Dr. Joseph P. Brennan. There were several grocery stores including John W. Dyer's east end Dyer & Co. Grocery and the Cash Market on Court Street. The People's Warehouse, established by Leon Cohen and Leo Falck in 1881, seemed to be an early version of today's outlet stores. Early banks included the First National (1881), the Pendleton Savings Bank, the Oregon Building and Loan Association (1888), the Pendleton National Bank (1881) and the Inland Empire Bank, which opened in 1919.

In 1920, Pendleton had a population of 7,387 people, an approximate increase of 3,000 in ten years. In 1921, G.A. Hartman served as mayor and E.B. Aldrich edited Pendleton's *East Oregonian*. In 1922, ten churches served the Christian Community, including the First Baptist (1876), the Episcopal Church (1872), United Methodists (1871), St. Mary's Catholic Church (1884), Presbyterian Church (1885), Peace Lutheran (1892), First Christian Church (1893), Christian Science (1904), Jehovah's Witness(1907) and a Seventh Day Adventist congregation that moved from Echo to Pendleton in 1922. Eight physicians practiced in the city, with Dr. Joseph P. Brennan associating with Dr. Frank E. Boyden at offices on Court Street. In 1922, Dr. Brennan helped Dr. Boyden organize the medical staff at St. Anthony's hospital and became active in the Umatilla County Medical Society. A couple of decades earlier, a group of Catholic sisters, headed by Mother Stanislaus, wanted to start a hospital. Dr. Frederick W. Vincent, active in the business community, donated $250 and suggested that she find "20 other crazy Irishmen to give a like amount." She succeeded in the fund raising effort, which was the beginning of St. Anthony's. Dr. Vincent, who served as Pendleton's mayor from 1879 to 1901, led the effort to build the first levee for flood control, helped develop the city's water works and pioneered the establishment of Pendleton's first power and light company. He served 30 years with the Union Pacific Railroad. In 1913, the state opened Eastern Oregon State Hospital in Pendleton, which brought a stable payroll to the area.

Pendleton got its first public high school in 1888. The three-story structure with a central tower served the district until replaced in 1912 by the John Murray Building. In 1904, Superintendent of Schools Walter Pierce raised approximately $60,000.00 to build three elementary schools in Pendleton; the Westside, Lincoln and East Side schools. Walter Pierce became Oregon's 17th Governor (after statehood), serving from January 8, 1923 to January 10, 1927. (Please see "Notes," p. 263.)

Pendleton Woolen Mills ca 1909

Pendleton Woolen Mills has been producing blankets, rugs and other woven wool products since the mid-1890s. Photo courtesy of Pendleton Woolen Mills.

The Golden Rule Hotel

According to Pioneer Trails, *the Golden Rule "featured steam heat, electric lights, courteous treatment and reasonable rates with special attention given to farmers and stockmen."*

Historic Pendleton Buildings

Top left: The courthouse, built in 1888, served Umatilla County until replaced in 1954. Top right: The East Oregonian Building. Edwin Aldrich became sole owner of the East Oregonian in 1913. Bottom left: The former Bi-Jou saloon at Main and Emigrant. The building next right held the Empire Meat Company. Pendleton's underground tour takes visitors under this build-ing. Bottom right: The Sophie (Byer) McComas' home in Pendleton.   *All photos this page (except the Byer's home), Matt Johnson, Howdyshell Studio, Pendleton; Byers home, the author.*

The People's Warehouse Block

From left, the People's Warehouse (1883), H.F. Johnson & Co. pharmacy, Jacob Frazer's building, housing Alexander & Co., the Pendleton National Bank (1881) and the Pendleton Hotel.

Union Oil Company ca 1922

Pendleton's Union Oil Company, "Best All Ways," met the needs of the early motorists, including those who traveled east on the Oregon Trail Highway or west on the new Columbia River Highway.   *Photos, Matt Johnson, Howdyshell Studio, Pendleton.*

Til Taylor

On July 25, 1920, Til Taylor, Sheriff of Umatilla County, was murdered by six convicts in a jail escape. He is remembered by the people of Umatilla County.   *Photo courtesy of Peg Willis.*

Pendleton Grain Growers Elevator

Hamley & Company

The Pendleton Grain Growers Old Wooden Elevator (left) was located on the CRH through Pendleton. The Hamley & Company store (right) has served the community for more than 100 years.   *Photo (left) courtesy of Peg Willis; Photo (right) the author.*

The Pendleton Round-Up

Above: Lorena Trickey, Champion Cowgirl Rider, 1922 Pendleton Round-Up. Elected to the National Cowboy Hall of Fame. Below: Bill Clark, champion bucking-bronco cowboy rides "Winnemucca."

Top photo courtesy of Steve Lehl; Bottom photo, Matt Johnson, Howdyshell studio, Pendleton.

Sources

Books:

Abbott, Carl, *Portland, Gateway to the Northwest*, 1997.

Abraham, Eleanor, *Reflections*, Compiled and published by the Eleanor Abraham, Rainier, Oregon.

Johansen, Dorothy O., *Empire of the Columbia*, Harper & Row, New York City, New York, 1967.

Lancaster, Samuel C., *The Columbia, America's Great Highway*, 2nd Edition, 1926.

Lockley, Fred, et al, *History of the Columbia River Valley from The Dalles to the Sea*, 3 Volumes, The S.J. Clarke Publishing Company, Chicago, Illinois, 1928.

MacNab, Gordon, *East Oregonian*, East Oregonian Publishing Company, Pendleton, Oregon, 1975.

Metteer, Olive, *Mary's Story*, The Optimist Printers, The Dalles, Oregon, 1971.

Rees, Helen Guyton, *Fairview, On Duck Lane*, Self-published, Fairview, OR, 1988.

Spatz, Dan (editor) with Rodger Nichols, *A Sesquicentennial History of Wasco County*, The Dalles Chronicle, The Dalles, 2004.

Umatilla County Historical Society, *Umatilla County: A Backward Glance*, E.O. Master Printers, Pendleton, 1980.

Various, *Fourth, Fifth, Sixth, Seventh and Eighth Biennial Reports of the State Highway Commission*, Salem Oregon, 1920, 1922, 1924, 1926 and 1928.

Watts, James Loring, *History of Scappoose, Oregon*, Scappoose Historical Society, third printing, Scappoose, Oregon, 2004.

Weatherford, Marion T., *Arlington, Child of the Columbia*, Oregon Historical Society, Portland, Oregon, 1977.

Organizations:

Columbia County Historical Society, St. Helens Oregon.

Crown Point Country Historical Society, P.O. Box 17, Bridal Veil, Oregon.

Oregon Department of Transportation (specifically, Robert Hadlow), Region 1, 123 NW Flanders, Portland, OR, 97209.

Scappoose Historical Society, Vivian Urie, President, Watts House, Scappoose, Oregon

Umatilla County Historical Society, *Pioneer Trails*, Volume 1, No. 2; Volume 2, No. 2; Volume 5, No. 1; Volume VI, No.4; Volume VII, No. 1; Volume 18, No.2; and Volume 21, No. 2.

Umatilla (city) Museum, Jodi LaCourisiere, Director, 911 Sixth Street, Umatilla, Oregon. (541) 922-0209

Notes

1. Page 66: The Oregon Steam Navigation Company (OSN) became the Oregon Railroad and Navigation Company (O R & N) in 1879. The Union Pacific Railroad became a major stockholder in 1889, but lost control in 1894. The line re-organized as the Oregon Railroad and Navigation Company (O RR & N) in 1896. The Union Pacific regained control near the turn of the century. The line became the Oregon-Washington Railroad and Navigation Company (O W R & N) in 1910, which lasted until the 1930s, when it was integrated into the Union Pacific.

2. Page 89: The ten restaurants are: The Royal Chinook (1924), The Corbett Cafe (1925), The Wayfarer Inn (mid-1920s), Chanticleer Inn (1912), View Point Inn (1925), Crown Point Chalet (1915), Johnson's Vista Cafe (early 1920s), Falls Chalet (1914), Latourell Villa (1915) and The White Elephant (date not known).

3. Page 258: All non-attributed quotes in this section come from the pamphlets, *Pioneer Trails* (above), published by the Umatilla County Historical Society, Pendleton, Oregon.

Useable Sections of the Historic Columbia River Highway

From Troutdale, the HCRH is driveable to Warrendale, where its joins I-84. This section provides access to:

1. Dabney State Park (day use) - 3.6 miles E of Troutdale's City Hall on the HCRH

2. Portland Women's Forum State Scenic Viewpoint - 9.2 miles E of Troutdale

3. Crown Point and the Vista House - 10.3 miles E of Troutdale (3 miles E of Corbett)

4. Guy W. Talbot State Park - 12.5 miles E of Troutdale

5. Shepperd's Dell State Natural Area - 13.9 miles E of Troutdale

6. Bridal Veil Falls State Scenic Viewpoint - 14.8 miles E of Troutdale

7. Wahkeena Falls - 18.1 miles E of Troutdale

8. Multnomah Falls - 18.6 miles E of Troutdale

9. Oneonta Creek and the Oneonta Bluff Tunnel - 20.8 miles E of Troutdale

10. Horsetail Falls - 21.1 miles E of Troutdale

11. Ainsworth State Park (camping) - 23 miles E of Troutdale

12. John B. Yeon State Scenic Corridor - 26 miles E of Troutdale

At Bonneville exit 41 provides access to the HCRH State Trail, which leads west to the Moffett Creek Bridge or east around Wauna Point, across Eagle Creek and on into Cascade Locks. The reverse of the route can be reached via exit 44 at Cascade Locks.

At Hood River (exit 64), the HCRH can be accessed off of Highway 35. The Hood River loops are driveable and lead to the Mark O. Hatfield HCRH State Trail. A visitor center is located at the west entry to the trail. From Mosier (exit 69), the trail follows the HCRH west through the twin tunnels to the visitor center (the reverse route).

From Mosier, the HCRH is driveable into The Dalles. East out of Mosier (from I-84 exit 69) highway 30 climbs to the Rowena Plateau, which provides a scenic viewpoint of the Rowena Loops and the Columbia River. The highway descends off the plateau via the loops, passes through the small settlement of Rowena and continues into The Dalles. The Discovery Center at The Dalles is accessed from the HCRH between Rowena and The Dalles via Discovery Drive. Another route to reach the Discovery Center (from I-84) is to use exit 82 to reach the HCRH, then turn west (parallel to the freeway) to Discovery Drive.

Though not part of the Historic Columbia River Highway, as currently defined, some sections of the old highway can be accessed (Columbia County, see pages 23 and 151-152; Umatilla County, see pages 245-258).

Index

Symbols

Wilson, Sam 181
wire trail 1, 75, 76
Wiser, William 67
Wood, John 228
Woodard, Barney 73
Woodle, Claude 76
Woodle's Hardware, Corbett 82
Wright, Colonel George 180
Wyeth, Nathaniel J. 32

Y

Yakima War 180
Yellept, Chief 230
Yeon, John B. 3, 51, 63
Yount, President Robert
    Columbia County Good Roads Association 4

Z

Z.F. Moody Warehouse Company 202
Zimmerman, Jacob 63
Zimmerman, Mr.
    Zimmerman, Isobel 64